Wisdom From Beyond

from our loving Universe

Blessings,
Connie

H. Constance Hill

Diamond Clear Vision

Copyright © 2011 by H. Constance Hill.

All rights reserved. No part of this book may be reproduced in any mechanical, photographic, or electronic process, or in the form of a phonographic recording; nor may it be stored in a retrieval system, transmitted, or otherwise be copied for public or private use, other than for "fair use" as brief quotations embodied in articles or reviews, without prior written permission of the publisher.

Cover Art and Soul Portraits copyright © 2011 by H. Constance Hill
Book design by Pamela Marin-Kingsley, Far-Angel Design

Published by Diamond Clear Vision
an imprint of Illumination Arts LLC.
140 Adams Street, Quincy, MA 02169

Internet: www.diamondclearvision.com
E-mail: info@diamondclearvision.com

If you are unable to order this book from your local bookseller, you may order directly from the publisher. Special quantity discounts for organizations are available.

Library of Congress Control Number: 2010935404

ISBN: 978-0-9829225-2-1

First hardcover Printing

Printed in the United States of America, on 30% PCW paper.

ECO-FRIENDLY BOOKS
Made in the USA

Dedicated to all those who by opening this book,

and themselves to a consideration of the wisdom within,

are demonstrating the curiosity and courage

that can lead to a new understanding and experience of life.

Contents

For **Y**our **I**nformation   1

Frequently **A**sked **Q**uestion**s**:   4

    What is an Entity?

    What does receiving a message from Spirit involve?

    What is your process of receiving messages from Spirit?

    Who decides which entities you receive messages from?

    How do you know that your work with Spirit is authentic?

    What are Soul Portraits?

    What if something I read in Wisdom From Beyond **doesn't ring true?**

Messages in response to the question: *What knowledge would you most like to pass along to humans living on Earth at this time?*

	Page		Page
Walt Disney	15	Martin Luther King, Jr.	74
Babe Ruth	18	Vincent van Gogh	77
Paul Newman	20	William James	81
Mother Teresa	22	Eleanor Roosevelt	86
Pope John Paul II	25	Frank Sinatra	88
Lady Diana	28	Fred Astaire	90
Leonard Bernstein	34	Mohandes Gandhi	93
Annie Oakley	37	Robert F. Kennedy	97
Edgar Cayce	40	Jesse James	100
Julia Child	45	Mary Cassatt	103
Albert Schweitzer	48	Dag Hammarskjöld	108
Arthur Fiedler	52	Winston Churchill	111
Ella Fitzgerald	55	Anne Frank	115
Samuel Clemens	58	John Lennon	119
Thomas Edison	61	Michael Jackson	122
Georgia O'Keeffe	64	Elvis Presley	124
Mary Baker Eddy	67	Elizabeth Kübler-Ross	127
Liberace	71		

Afterword   131

In Gratitude   133

About the Author   134

For Your Information

This book contains messages received by me from 35 personalities with names well-known to humans. As readers will immediately realize from reading the list of message-bearers in the *Contents*, all have passed on from Earth. Their messages have been communicated from the spiritual realm, where their lives continue. From a perspective now in Spirit, these *discarnate* (without a physical body) *entities* are aware of information that they know would help humans better understand life.

You may have heard the saying: "When a student is ready, a teacher will appear." Since this book has found its way into your hands, perhaps *you* are such a student. Certainly, the entities who have contributed to this volume are teachers, and they are delighted to be able to serve from afar. Their messages are a gathering of *Wisdom From Beyond* for all of us on Earth.

The idea for this book came suddenly one summer day, arriving as a complete concept. I knew I was to receive communications from a number of individuals with widely known names, all of whom had crossed over to Spirit relatively recently—within the past century or so! The message I would receive from each would be in answer to the question: **What knowledge would you most like to pass along to humans living on Earth at this time?**

FYI

I knew, too, that the messages were to come from such an intriguing group of personalities no longer on Earth, that seeing their names listed as contributors to the book would tempt many to look inside—even those who normally are not readers, or believers in the possibility of communication with Spirit. And, I knew, this book was one whose time had come, because those in Spirit who would deliver the messages believe that the information they have to offer is vital for humanity to have *now*.

Frequently Asked Questions

What is an Entity?

In *Wisdom From Beyond,* I use the term *entity* to describe a once *incarnated* (physically embodied) human with a specific personality in a specific lifetime on Earth, who has passed back to life in the spiritual realm. Returned to Spirit, this Self, while retaining its individuality, is a much more expanded being than it was as its former human personality.

Simply because it has returned to the spiritual realm, however, does not mean that an entity has become "enlightened." The journey to spiritual understanding usually takes many lifetimes. Nevertheless, being back in the higher vibration of Spirit does mean that an entity has regained knowledge of the eternal nature of Life. Thus, entities communicating from the perspective of the spiritual realm have an enlarged view of life to share with humans.

Returned to the realm of Spirit, entities have rejoined the *collective consciousness* of the Universe. On Earth, this usually is referred to as the *collective* **un***conscious.* In the higher vibrations, however, eternal Life is a fully conscious concept to all. There, the *Oneness* that unites all beings in the Universe is clear. It is this universal awareness that accounts for the similarities in many of the messages the entities have contributed to *Wisdom From Beyond.*

FAQs

What is Spirit?

As used in *Wisdom From Beyond*, the term *Spirit* refers to the non-physical realm of existence. Neither Spirit nor the spiritual realm is used here with any connection to "religion." Religion is an institutional creation of humans.

What does receiving a message from Spirit involve?

Only their vibrational rates differentiate beings on Earth from beings in Spirit. Humans in physical form have a lower frequency, which rises to a much higher one at the time they cross back to the spiritual realm.

Entities in Spirit who wish to connect with humans know that the widely differing vibrational rates between life on Earth and in the non-physical realm must be reconciled in order to make communication possible. A being in the spiritual realm must adjust its energy "down" in order to make contact with a person on Earth, who must, at the same time, raise his or her energy.

Humans who are open to this process are called *channels* or *mediums*. Those who are most effective at channeling and mediumship "set aside" their human egos in order to be fully focused on the communication coming from Spirit. They also set their intentions to be open only to energy which serves what is the highest and best for all concerned.

Although some humans spontaneously receive messages from energies in the spiritual realm, most who do so have responsibly prepared for this to happen. They have read materials that have been channeled by others, and studied in spiritual development groups. They have adapted their behavior on the physical plane in order to raise their vibrations. Such modifications include meditation, altered eating and drinking habits, spending more time in the natural world and, in general, focusing on people, places, and activities that have high vibes.

What is your process of receiving messages from Spirit?

When sitting to take communications from Spirit, I first set the intention to attract only energies that will serve the highest purpose. I do this through meditation and prayer forms that clear my energy. I then focus on connecting with those beings in Spirit who wish to contact me.

My message-taking process is as follows. With paper and pen in front of me I sit quietly, mentally asking for the entity that is most strongly connected to me in the present moment to identify itself and come into my energy field. I wait until I feel a "buzz" of energy at the top of my head, and sense a first word forming. I write that word down, and the next that arrives. Usually,

FAQs

the flow of communication then continues. My eyes are open as I write, and I am fully aware of my surroundings and what I am doing. I am *not* in trance. I remain focused and receptive to the information the entity is directing to me.

I do not "hear" (*clairaudience*) or "see" (*clairvoyance*) what is being communicated. Rather, I "sense" (*clairsentience*) the thoughts being "impressed" upon my mind. The best way I can describe what happens is that I "pull out" words and "assemble" sentences to faithfully record the information an entity is passing along to me. A part of my mind that feels "set aside" seems to oversee the process. I do not have a more precise description of what is happening - which may not be surprising, considering the nature of the experience!

When I feel a strong emphasis on what I am receiving, I use Initial Capital Letters, *italics,* or ***bold italics,*** to reflect the intensity of the entity's delivery. When channeling a message, I focus on writing as quickly as is necessary to keep up with the energy flow of the entity communicator. When an entity has completed its message, I feel a drop in the energy of the connection. I may also know that a message is concluded by an entity's closing words or sentiment.

On occasion, I recognize that, for whatever reason, the strength of the connection with an entity has weakened, even though the message dosen't feel complete. I have learned to accept this, and to stop the session at such a point, so that I will not be tempted to "make up" material that is not truly coming from the entity. Usually, in another session, the entity returns to finish the message or, sometimes, to add something quite unrelated.

Only later do I edit the message for spelling and grammar, and for sentence and paragraph structure, so that it will read clearly. Before editing, I again prepare myself with meditation and prayers. Often at this stage I feel the energy of the entity return, which allows me to confirm with it that the message I've written down is faithful to what it wishes to share with humans.

Who decides which entities you receive messages from?

The entities themselves do. After receiving the initial inspiration for *Wisdom From Beyond*, I couldn't resist making a list of the potential passed-on personalities that came to mind. Nevertheless, even at this early stage, I believe it was the entities themselves that were sending energetic impulses that resulted in me putting their names on the list.

From the first message I took for the book, I implemented a procedure to "distance" myself in the selection process. Once prepared to receive a message, I would close my eyes and allow my right index finger to hover above the list of names until it settled on one. I then wrote that name at the top of the paper in front of me, welcomed the entity, and waited for a message. I followed this pattern for the first dozen or so messages.

By that point, I had become aware intuitively that the original list of personalities was to be expanded. I remember the day a change occurred. After preparing to take a message, I sat before the paper with pen poised. After the buzz of energy in my head signaled that an entity had "entered," it was with delight that I received a very clear sense that the message-bearer-to-be was Liberace. My delight came from knowing that I myself never would have thought to include Liberace in *Wisdom From Beyond.* "His" appearance confirmed for me that the messages were, indeed, coming through on energies other than my own.

Thereafter, as I sat for messages, I "followed the energy." Some days, it was not until the second, third, or even fourth "energy" had identified itself to me that I felt a strength of contact sufficient to signify that this was the entity I would be receiving an actual message from that day. I came to realize that many entities simply enjoy discovering that they can "come through" to humans in this manner, and that there are many more that will be doing so in the future.

How do you know that your work with Spirit is authentic?

As grateful and joyful as I am to be a partner in this wonderful extra-terrestrial communication, when I first began working with the entities for *Wisdom From Beyond* I did sometimes wonder whether the messages really were coming from Spirit. Could they possibly be my imagination? I needed to answer this question for myself, as well as for future readers.

When I am receiving a message from an entity I also am tapping into the *collective consciousness* of the Universe. Because of this, I sometimes feel as if the ideas being communicated by the entities through me are in my own words. I have had to get used to working with the energy in the spiritual realm in order not to misinterpret this experience as one in which I am writing the messages myself.

Working consistently and over time with the wide variety of entity energies that have come to and through me with messages has provided a foundation of faith. Interacting regularly with the spiritual realm moved my energy from the ego of the mind to the intelligence of my heart. As I continued to open to spirit-inspired guidance, I became increasingly able to set aside any temptation to control the content of the messages. I found myself trusting my work with the entities, which made the process more efficient, effective, fun, and valuable for all.

As the message bearers from beyond continue to surprise and humble me with their expansive messages, I've become convinced that the communication connection with Spirit is authentic. The messages in *Wisdom From Beyond* speak unfailingly of love, healing, wholeness, Oneness, freedom from fear, and eternal Life. They are consistent with the constants of existence in the spiritual realm. That the information also is helpful for humans living on Earth is what, ultimately, will prove its truth and worth.

FAQs

What are Soul Portraits?

I have painted an original Soul Portrait for each entity that has contributed to *Wisdom From Beyond.* A Soul Portrait is a representation of the unique spark of divine energy that an entity—*and,* each one of us—truly is. Since an entity has passed back to its larger expression of eternal Life in the spiritual realm, a photograph of it, as the physical human being it was when incarnated on Earth, would no longer be an accurate depiction of its energy.

Each entity was pleased to sit for its Soul Portrait. This was no exhibition of ego. Rather, the entities intend these vivid color portrayals of their energy as healing, loving gifts to you from the spirit realm. Watercolor is the chosen medium for Soul Portraits because water and paint flowing together allow Spirit to "jump in" to create the highest possible vibration for the viewers' benefit.

Soul Portraits can be used to reflect upon after reading the entity's message, or as part of a meditation practice. While the entities confirmed the positioning of their portraits on the printed page, they encourage you to view the art from different angles in order to experience the complete energy of the images.

The Soul Portraits of humans carry healing gifts as well. In keeping with the energy of *Wisdom from Beyond,* a Soul Portrait of the author appears at the back of the book.

What if something I read in Wisdom From Beyond ***doesn't ring true?***

Pay attention to the information in the book that does resonate with you, to the ideas that feel helpful, "familiar," or about which you could say "That feels right to me." Notice how your mind, body, and spirit feel as you read this book. Allow anything that seems uncomfortable or negative simply to flow away.

There is no intention on the part of the entities, or me, to convince you what to believe. Follow what your heart tells you. *Always. You are your own authority.* When you encounter what does feel right, you will know what is true for you.

Messages

and

Soul Portraits

Walt Disney

As humans you are very special beings, and during life on Earth you experience unique opportunities. Much is said about the challenges of the density of Earth's vibrational field. But, it is this very quality that encourages humans to reach deeply into their own energy for creative expression. Creativity flows freely from the spiritual realm to those on Earth as they open to receive it. This requires an intention to do so on the part of humans, because of the difference in vibration between the realms.

The creative process, the empowering source of Life, aids humans in learning about their spiritual nature. It is in the experimenting with and expression of the higher vibrational creative energy that each human and, collectively, all humanity, is motivated toward spiritual evolution.

During sleep or meditative activities, when human consciousness (the ego) is set aside, creative ideas are received. These come from the great collective consciousness, although each transmission of creative energy to a specific human is expressed uniquely. The spiritual core within each person is capable of its own use and interpretation of this energy transmission. Each human is free to ignore it, of course, but the creative energy *is* there.

Humans who are open and curious will experience a free flow of creative "sparks." If these are recognized, and played and experimented with, they can lead to great inner fulfillment. Their expression in various forms also can offer pleasure and healing to others.

Walt Disney

What is most important for humans to realize is that *every person* has innate access to the Universal Creative Source. It is as available as the air you breathe. It is simply a matter of *choosing* to be receptive to it.

When you set your intention to align with the creative energy of the Universe—the same energy from which the Universe was created in the first place—you shift yourself from unconscious to conscious living. This is a very significant step in the evolution of a soul during earthly incarnation.

All souls were born in conscious connection with the Creative Source. However, when a soul makes a choice to incarnate on the earth plane—as I did as Walt Disney—awareness of this can be lost in the slower, lower vibrations on there. A human may, therefore, remain unconscious of its unique creativity until its life choices lead to an expanded awareness from which it can open to receive creative energy consciously.

From its birth on Earth, a human's spiritual guides always are introducing impulses to open awareness to this creative energy. Those humans with more awareness—perhaps gained in previous incarnations—may open to their creative selves earlier in a given lifetime than others. However, do know that ***all*** can foster their own creative awareness and expression by applying intention and attention.

Since every thought and every action is a creative choice, paying attention to all daily expressions leads a human along the path to realizing its soul's creative potential and joy. This is nothing more—and nothing less—than becoming the Being you were created to be. ❖

Babe Ruth

Wisdom from Beyond

George Herman "Babe" Ruth

Play ball! This is one of the main occupations I had in the earthly incarnation as Babe Ruth. To play ball when I did, and as I did, was not necessarily fun much of the time. My career as a baseball professional did not feel like "play." Not really; not in my soul.

The pressures and responsibilities might, from the outside, have appeared to be less than those of someone working in an office, in the insurance industry for example, but no human ever truly knows what another is experiencing. And that's why every human being on the earth plane, if he or she could see into the souls of others, would feel nothing but compassion and love for every other person.

All who incarnate on Earth take on the dense, cumbersome energy of physical bodies—yes, even athletes—to learn lessons of the soul. Whatever the lessons may be that a human has set for itself, it is always to be hoped that in the course of the learning, growth in compassion will be prominent.

Paul Newman

Paul Newman

I had no idea when I was incarnated as Paul Newman on Earth that life energy passed so freely across the vibrational realms. Although my energy is only recently returned to the higher vibration of Spirit (**Note:** *Paul Newman communicated this message just one month following his transition to Spirit*) I am so intrigued by this knowledge that I wanted to experiment with this form of communication as soon as I became aware of an opportunity. Thank you for allowing me to continue to learn, and perhaps now to teach, others from beyond.

My early impression of the Spirit world, with its vast community of souls not presently incarnated, is of the enormous vitality, creativity, and love that is the reality here. All who pass over from Earth return to this energy. Some have a healing period after arrival—if that is for their highest good—before exploring more fully the opportunities that await here.

Upon return to Spirit, a soul finds that all which brought harmless pleasure to it while on the physical plane is available here. I send word to Joanne (**Note:** *Joanne Woodward, his wife on Earth*) that there are racing vehicles here! However, the opportunities in Spirit are so varied that most souls seem to "stretch their wings," so to speak, and expand their choice of activities once they become re-acclimated to the higher vibration.

I wanted to get the message out to human beings on Earth right away to let them know not only that life continues after "death," but how full and fascinating ongoing existence is once the return home to Spirit is accomplished.

Mother Teresa

Wisdom from Beyond

Mother Teresa

It is a pleasure to be in the Earth energy field again as I communicate here. I was given credit for being "saintly" during the final years of my incarnation as Mother Teresa. However, when one is doing the work, the service, which one has chosen for oneself to accomplish in a given physical lifetime, following that path is truly a joy. It is the fulfilling of one's soul, and the discussion of being a "saint" doesn't enter into the matter.

I loved my life as Mother Teresa. The sense of fulfillment that arose in me from being in a community of like-hearted fellow workers, and the sharing of my spirit with those who were so appreciative of the loving, healing care that was offered to them in a manner which they could receive without guilt or shame, was deeply enriching. It was an experience of awareness of the Universe's true state of *Oneness.*

We are all One. Which is to say that each being on Earth, indeed, every being in the Universe, is connected through the similarity of feelings that flow through all hearts. When feelings are flowing freely in a human's heart, an increasing awareness builds. It is an awareness of the truth of the Universe: that **Love** is the only energy that exists.

There is much talk on Earth at this time about "energy sources." If individual humans could come to the understanding that the only true energy in the Universe is **Love**, humanity as a whole would discover that there is more than enough water, food, and fuel for everyone—with resources to spare.

Mother Teresa

It is a matter of allowing one's self to become aware that there is *never* a need for fear. Fear is the very opposite of love. Fear—or anger, hate, greed, and all fear's other outgrowths—closes the human heart. Because the "heavy" energy on Earth does not naturally have the lightness of Love, it can take humans a long time to become aware of its full power.

It may take lifetimes, and usually does, for the knowledge of the true strength of **Love**—incredibly gentle, yet powerful beyond all imagination—even to begin to be comprehended by human beings. However, there are now on Earth an increasing number who are moving into such an awareness. As more and more humans are presented with opportunities to reach an expanded understanding of **Love**, and as they find communities of similarly-minded people who are moving toward living in a new state of Being, Earth will change.

There is much discussion of the changes that are coming to the Earth at this time. While many people are fearful of potential happenings, the truth is that the changes can be positive ones, ones which the Earth very much needs **Now**.

As one example: With the movement towards a greater awareness in humans of **Love**, feelings and actions of nationalism will lose the fierceness that leads to war. Then, fears of lacks of water, food, and fuel, will lead instead to planning across national borders to ensure that basic needs for all are met.

Wisdom from Beyond

Pope John Paul II

PAX. The heart that is at peace helps heal the whole Universe.

While I was on Earth, especially as I moved toward the position as Pope John Paul II, I was enmeshed in a life of religious dogma, with rules that concerned the souls of others. As I progressed through the political hierarchy of the Roman Catholic Church in that earthly incarnation, in many ways, strange as it may seem, I moved away from my own soul's evolution.

Yes, I occasionally was able to be a shepherd to the worldwide Roman Catholic flock. But, more often, it felt as if I was judge and jury, the enforcer of regulations for what amounted to a multinational corporation. Sometimes, it felt as if that corporation was soulless.

From within the Roman Catholic Church, I had glimpses of the spiritual realm to which we *all* return after an earthly incarnation. It was not, however, until I had actually passed to Spirit, and regained the perspective on Life that a soul has from here, that I again truly felt the higher vibrations of fully loving energy. In Spirit, unconditional love is known to be available to all. On Earth, this precious universal heritage is falsely believed by many to reside solely with the clergy and ecclesiastical officials.

What is true, as I see it now, is that *every soul is a living expression of Love.* It is important for you on Earth to know this, and that is why I am speaking of these things to you now, in this way. For, it is important for humans to know that life is an eternal passage during which their soul chooses varied experiences that will help make this essential knowledge about love ever more clear.

Pope John Paul II

Humans can contribute to their soul growth during earthly incarnations by expanding their understanding of what Life truly is. *Life is for joyfully following the natural flow of the heart's intelligence.* The human heart has a "brain." This "heart brain"—which some scientists on Earth now acknowledge—better serves a human than the "mind brain," which has been highly regarded for so long.

The mind brain is keeper of the manmade rules and regulations accepted by humans. It is the heart brain, however, that connects to the natural and spiritual laws that truly apply on Earth, as well as in the millions, nay billions, of other living environments for souls in the Universe.

Society on Earth, which has both delights and challenges unique in the Universe, requires laws and governance because of the extreme range in soul evolution found there. What humans can benefit from most,—if they are able to hear and consider this—is that **each human, each soul, truly is its own keeper. There is no outside authority** in any religious, governmental or other institution **that can evolve your soul for you**. Only with the *inner* work of becoming your own authority will your soul develop.

A human, when it is willing to listen deeply within itself, eventually moves into the *inner knowingness* that it is its own authority. The true teacher of a soul is not a priest, a guru, or the Pope. It is your own dear Self, which is a unique particle of the Creator of the Universe.

Lady Diana

Wisdom from Beyond

Lady Diana

I learned many lessons in my earthly incarnation as Diana Spenser, later Diana, Princess of Wales. Life on the physical plane is a challenging school for most who undertake it. It requires much courage at many points during each incarnation in order to accomplish the lessons a soul sets for itself while still in the higher vibrational realm before undertaking an Earth experience.

In Spirit, a soul is quite conscious of working with its masters, teachers, and guides to set tasks and arrange the incidences and challenges from which it can learn. Once on Earth, it must master the desired lessons so thoroughly in the slow physical energy there that they are learned for all time. This is one of the "gifts" of the Earth school.

However, a soul in Spirit "mapping out" a physical life path can't properly take into account the "forgetfulness" that takes place once it is in the dense Earth energy. It is this forgetting of the spiritual realm and its laws that accounts for the real challenge of earthly life. During its portion of life on Earth a soul can forget even the most basic truths of the Universe: **_Life is eternal; Love is the energy that powers Life; and there is no cause for shame or blame as Life's lessons are learned._**

Another law is that _each human creates by his or her own freewill choices the life it experiences on Earth._ Yes, there is a reckoning for one's choices, but it is a very forgiving and encouraging accounting, meant only to foster further learning. Know that every soul eventually will reach _Enlightenment:_ the complete understanding of the _Oneness of Life_, the knowledge that all beings are connected in a beautiful web of Love.

Lady Diana

Some take longer to arrive at this understanding than others, perhaps needing many, many, many lifetimes. But *all* will eventually arrive at the same wonderful destination. Until then, between physical incarnations, they are nourished and rehabilitated in the higher vibrations, each being taught, *and* teaching.

I, fairly typically in my earthly experience as Diana, forgot as that human life progressed the sense of connection with all beings that I had arrived on Earth knowing. During late childhood, I experienced a "forgetting" that left me feeling isolated from the spiritual realm, alone and struggling with the challenges of life on the physical plane.

In Spirit, I had chosen for my incarnation as Diana what many humans would call a privileged upbringing in British nobility. But, that means little to a child when there also is loneliness, a feeling of abandonment. I lived in a shadow of invisibility, despite an outer appearance of prosperity. I created an inner life for myself, but could not reach the true security of my soul. There were no humans around with the insight that would have comforted me. In truth, I had chosen a challenging childhood to move through that earthly life's learning.

The phase of my human incarnation for which I am most remembered began when I was still quite young, unformed in many of my beliefs. I met Charles, Prince of Wales, when I was an impressionable young teenager. Over the next few years, pressure mounted on him to marry, since it was particularly important for him to produce an heir to the throne of the United Kingdom. Charles and I came closer together under those circumstances.

As large a stage as we were playing on, and as glamorous a one as it seemed at times, human existence comes down to feelings and the personal experience of them. Basically, we were just two people trying to sort out our feelings for each other. Media exposure made that attempt all but impossible, certainly for such a relatively sheltered young lady as I had been. It took a sadly short time for me, a 19-year-old, to become immersed in the carefully-controlled adult world of the British Court, where there was so very much more involved than the personal happiness of two people, who might or might not be "in love," compatible, or even suitable.

Beyond the Court intrigue and massive protocol education which I was subjected to—of necessity, I absolutely understood—there was, as I got to know Charles, the awareness that his adult life already had been going on for a number of years. It had evolved in many aspects long before he knew I was alive, from the perspective of potential spouse.

All the while there continued to be an intense education on the manners and mores of what was probably the most formal social structure on Earth. At first, I was treated with curiosity and consideration both within the palace and without. Increasingly, however, this turned to inconsideration, and even aggression, in the stark reality of the far-reaching glare of celebrity. To live under that spotlight took more strength of character and courage than hardly anyone could come close to imagining.

Life grew more difficult. Of course, there was wealth, glamour, travel, and contact with other famous, rich, and royal. So often, though, I just wanted to sit across the table from my husband for dinner. However, we couldn't. We didn't.

The birth of my first son William thrilled both of us and, seemingly, the whole world—though, always, there was worry for the safety of such a world-famous baby. Really, if people

Lady Diana

truly could envision the compromises that existence in the circle of such celebrity incurs, I can't imagine a single soul choosing to experience it.

The most precious hours of my life as Diana were spent in the company of my sons, the *very best moments* being those when we were alone together. Having children was a soul goal for me, and I achieved it, though in a distorted kind of family life.

I *was* grateful to my celebrity when it enabled me to more effectively support charities and other service missions. Because of who I was, I was able to elicit others' help and thus enlarge the circles of aid, each radiating out to help more people. I was honored, and humbled, to understand this influence in my days as Diana, Princess of Wales, and sought to make the highest and best use of my position.

Practically the only persons I had a genuinely intimate sharing with—partly because of their precious innocence—were my sons, William and Harry. Most other relationships, from the time of my engagement to Charles forward, were much complicated by my role as "Princess of Wales," no matter how much I sought to avoid the intrusion of that title.

Without dwelling on details, I came to find the demands of my life difficult. The unreal air of celebrity left me feeling as if I was always sitting in front of a mirror. I found myself so exhausted that I decided to take one of "the exits back to Spirit" that a soul always writes into its script for a human incarnation. I knew that my choosing to exit human life would seem tragic in the outer world—though passing back to Spirit never is truly tragic for the soul crossing over. My soul was ready for the blessing of returning home.

I agonized over leaving William and Harry so young, but I didn't feel I had much left to give them. I knew Charles would continue to be an excellent and loving father to them in the years ahead. I realized, too, that the celebrity that had often been so painful to me during life on Earth would, as a result of the dramatic circumstances of my passing, provide a tremendous last boost of good for the charities to which I had been devoted.

I am alive—I am at peace—I send Love to all on Earth.

❖

Leonard Bernstein

Wisdom from Beyond

Leonard Bernstein

While I was on the earth plane as Leonard Bernstein I loved the song line: *"The hills are alive with the sound of music."* Having passed over, I can report that the spiritual realm is alive with the sound of music, alive with the joy of music. I relish the feeling of being surrounded by its energy, and so does every soul here, not just those of us who were devoted to music in an earthly incarnation.

Music is a healing form here. It is on Earth also, as some enlightened practitioners know. Humans who work with and teach music are aware that some combinations and progressions of notes carry within them healing energies. Often, such sequences are found in classical music "classics." The so-called New Age music, with its less "resolved" compositional style, also is very healing. It helps free the brain to float in different streams of sound which replicate the musical healing modalities we access on the spiritual plane.

I support creativity in all its forms, on Earth and in Spirit. Therefore, the subsequent statement I shall make is not meant to stifle the free expression of musical form. However, it is important for me to offer humans on Earth the following information. Some of the contemporary music that is currently popular on Earth does not carry the qualities that give music its gift of healing energy. For example, the "heavy" energy of the music that goes by the name heavy metal—which I literally can see from my present perspective in Spirit—does not.

Leonard Bernstein

    I am not suggesting that humans who wish to experience such music forms avoid them all together. I simply suggest that they balance their choices with lighter and brighter musical works in order to receive the healing benefit these carry.
    Higher, lighter, energy forms in general are much stronger than dense, heavier ones. This holds true for music, so even a short exposure to music that offers healing qualities can counteract music styles which lack them. If you open yourself to the many diverse instrumental and vocal styles on Earth that are healing, your soul *will* resound with the sound of music.

Annie Oakley

As the human incarnation named Annie Oakley I lived on Earth in tumultuous times. *Tumultuous times*. I am speaking in particular of inner tumult. I came to physical life to express myself as a *large* energy. Although both male and female energy could express itself with strength in the time and society in which I incarnated, it was more usual then for a woman to show her strength in domestic and familial roles, while a man could be out in the world more openly. My inner being longed for a diverse experience of human life. I was guided to actions and skills that enabled me to create an adventure that satisfied this soul desire.

What I learned in my life as Anne Oakley was that, to be truly fulfilled, there is a need for balance. Fulfillment results from outward action balanced with inner reflection. As Annie Oakley, I did not spend much energy on cultivating inner awareness, and thus was never truly at peace in that life, or satisfied with its apparent accomplishments. "If I had my life to live over…" is a sentiment we in Spirit often hear humans voice. In truth, human beings *must* live lives over and over, and over, until they learn the lessons they need to master.

What further wisdom I gained from examining my life as Annie Oakley from the perspective of Spirit is that I would have benefited from spending more time alone with myself appreciating the natural world. I often was close to nature in that life, but largely ignored it for the clamor and glamour of frontier towns and cosmopolitan cities. I sought to be a "sensational act," as Annie Oakley certainly proved to be in both North America and Europe.

Annie Oakley

When humans come to realize that life does not end with their physical death—nor begin with physical birth into an incarnation—they will be able, while still on Earth, to take a *larger* view of their experiences. With such awareness, they will gain a larger-than-THIS-lifetime perspective for reflecting upon the balance of mind, body, and spirit.

Edgar Cayce

Edgar Cayce

I am very pleased to be connecting with the Earth plane at this time. It is rather a reversal of roles for me to be the energy in Spirit communicating with a human channel on Earth, and I am truly pleased to experience this other side of the situation!

From a perspective in the higher vibrations, I know that communication across the realms is quite common. I can also report that for everyone on Earth who seeks this contact *with good intentions* there are many in Spirit who are *ready and waiting* to connect with them. There is the matter of adjusting the respective vibrations so that the communication will be intelligible. Energy in Spirit adapts its higher vibration "down" in order to reach a being on Earth.

Once a human believes this sort of communication is possible, and thus is open to the exchange, it is only a matter of consistent intention and effort to accomplish the connection. Belief that such an exchange is possible generally involves a human who has achieved a degree of awareness of spiritual and natural law.

Sometimes, though, as was the case with me in my earthly incarnation as Edgar Cayce, communication with Spirit can begin spontaneously, without any conscious intent. When a connection has taken this form, if the human subsequently continues to communicate with Spirit, it often does so by entering a "trance" state, and is not completely aware of what is transpiring while in that state. It is imperative when the communication takes place in trance that the human participant has a trusted human helper with whom it is comfortable and able to relax.

At the human stage during which I did most of my "readings," trance work was more common than it is now. The energy on Earth was different then, and the disparity between the higher and lower vibrations of Spirit and earth plane greater. It usually only could be bridged by a human entering a trance state. The vibration on Earth has risen since I did trance work there. This change began in earnest with the beginning of the Age of Aquarius, near the end of what is known on Earth as the 20th century.

With the rise of the energetic vibration on Earth, it is now not as challenging to bridge the vibrational gap. The greater number of humans who are opening to an awareness of spiritual communication forms such as "channeling" and "mediumship" represent a significant advancement. Trance work takes quite a toll on the human body, eventually wearing it out, as it did mine. Thus, it is a great improvement for humans to be able to contact entities in the spirit realms through mental intention rather than physical trance.

I observe with interest the manner of health care on planet Earth at the present time. My "intuitive" medical readings were among the most unexpected and valued segments of my work with humans. I must say that I am surprised, in some ways, that there is not more intuitive medical work being done on Earth now. After all, for an attuned medical intuitive there is no need for years and years of expensive education in medical schools, an education that often proves quickly out-dated—sometimes even by the time it is being taught—because the energy of the Earth plane currently is changing so rapidly.

Medical intuitives—and there are a number in practice on Earth today, though nowhere nearly enough—can override the low vibration of Earth's traditional mindset of learning. Its low energy often holds back new medical information from coming to Earth because the human intellect rejects out-of-hand most modalities that lack the narrowly conceived supporting data that the scientific establishment —and many patients themselves—yet insist upon. When resistance to alternative thinking within the medical professions and the greed mentality present in segments of the medical and pharmaceutical industries diminish, there will be many advances in healing for humans.

I wish to take note of, and support, the many humans in the health care professions who are open to the energies that create new concepts for well-being and treatment. Often, these are renewed ideas, really, since many of those that are truly helpful have been extant since the beginning of human evolution. Sadly, such awareness "beyond the book" remains extremely limited in certain places on Earth. And, the resources that exist, including financial funding, often are used in most inappropriate and ineffective ways.

Such is the nature of the dense energy on Earth that "things take time." Nevertheless, although still happening mostly behind-the-scenes in the energetic realms, changes *are* now taking place.

Every human who assumes more responsibility for its own well-being will be well served. *Follow your heart, follow your feelings, emotional as well as physical, rather than your mind. This is sound advice in any circumstance on Earth, but never more significantly so than in your care of your body, the cocoon for your soul during human incarnations.*

Edgar Cayce

As humans expand their willingness to examine their lives and make choices that are positive for their own physical systems, their awareness in all aspects of life will open. Then, their earthly lives, short as these segments are in the scope of Eternal Life, will be more healthy, peaceful, joyful, and loving.

❖

Wisdom from Beyond

Julia Child

Bon appetit! Here in the higher vibrational realms, where I have shed the physical body that was Julia Child on Earth for the much more joyful form of Spirit, there is no need to eat food to sustain life. You might think that this is an unhappiness for me, but not so! I can spend my energy nourishing myself with the many other alternative delights available here.

True, food is one of the sensual pleasures that those spirits incarnating once again on the earth plane may look forward to, a compensation for the soul while it is in physical form. Yet, the joys in Spirit are universally held here in the higher vibrations to be vastly more satisfying than physical ones. And, a soul, as it readies to depart its human form and physical life on Earth, is well-aware of the joys to which it is returning. In other words, I don't miss the lack of food here!

During much of their development on Earth, humans focus on the physical senses. Eventually, however, in the course of *soul evolution*, even humans on Earth realize that the world of the non-physical is far more satisfying—and **never boring**, if any of you readers are thinking that!

Life in the spiritual realm as it truly is is so expansive, so interesting, *so thrilling in all its aspects*—there really are no words to convey this to the human mind—that there never is any longing for Earth on the part of a soul once it has returned to Spirit. There *is* a recognition by those returned to the spiritual realm of the emotions felt by their dear ones who yet remain

Julia Child

on Earth, and of their grief concerning the seeming "loss" of the departed soul. While the entity that has returned to Spirit is aware of such longings, it also knows that these will dissolve once those on Earth make their own transition back to Spirit .

All souls returning to Spirit regain knowledge of the truth of existence: *Humans really are eternal spiritual beings having a temporary life experience in physical form.* From my perspective I say to you: Hallelujah for that!

❖

Albert Schweitzer

Wisdom from Beyond

Albert Schweitzer

Earth is smaller today than ever, due to transportation methods and technology. And overpopulation has shrunk the available pool of resources, especially since various members of the human race practice hoarding. Because the world is shrinking, it is incumbent upon *every* human to become more aware of, and caring toward, every other being on the planet. This is the *only* way that human life will be able to continue to exist.

It really *is* true that there is nothing to fear but your own fears, and the fears of others. *Fear closes the human heart, to oneself, as well as others. When you are able to care, when you have released fear, you can use the resources in your life—energy, time, water, food—more consciously.* A fear-free approach to living, once a human has espoused it, reaches across the boundaries of nationhood, and political, religious, racial, and socio-economic identification, to an acknowledgement that all Life is One.

Earth is made weaker by each species that is lost to the pollution of so-called progress. Every species, including plants and insects, has gifts for Life. When a species becomes extinct, those gifts are gone. The Universe is diminished by such unnecessary loss.

As they become aware of the interconnectedness of all Life, humans also open to a realization of the sacredness of each member of their own species. Every human is a unique portion of the creative energy of the Universe. As such, each is an essential individual spark of Life.

It is incumbent upon humans to recognize the preciousness of each being on Earth. *The act of opening one's heart to each and every other physical creature is the surest and swiftest course of action in the salvation of Earth.*

Albert Schweitzer

In the earthly life in which I incarnated as Albert Schweitzer, I spent much time in Africa, rural Africa. Life in rural Africa was then, and remains today, very different from the cosmopolitan European culture in which I grew up and was educated. I was guided to the African experiences to fulfill the intention I had set for myself in that incarnation. This was to learn about *the Oneness of Life*, the bond between all beings, human and other, and the Earth itself. The African experiences I was offered—and claimed—were a perfect laboratory in which my ideas and ideals about the Oneness of the world could grow.

At the time I lived in Africa, political independence and technology were less present than they are now. Yet, my learning, even though it took place in a poor, rural arena, was broader and offered more engagement with Life's lessons than many humans living in today's cosmopolitan cities would think possible.

What I want to impart from the spiritual realm is that *in whatever circumstances a human finds itself on Earth,* **there** *is where an opportunity exists to grow in an appreciation that all Life is intimately interrelated.* It is as you have heard: "Bloom where you are planted." The natural world does this without questioning.

Earth, or *Gaia*, balances itself according to its need to provide the necessities for *all* Life. From a human perspective this can look less than benign, in terms of storms, earthquakes, floods or famine. Yet, these are necessary balancings in order for Life as we know it to continue. As more humans move to a deeper understanding of Oneness, by raising their consciousnesses about the uses of their lives, there may be less need for the aspects of "balancing" by Earth that appear "tragic" to humans.

From insect to whale, blade of grass to towering tree, the natural world is the foundation of Earth, present long before the appearance of the human species. As Albert Schweitzer, I was blessed with opportunities to learn about the proper role for humans on Earth—which embodies more life forms than humans can comprehend. It is in developing humility through life experiences that an awareness of Oneness arises.

Every aspect of existence is a vital component that contributes to the whole. The journey toward appreciating the Oneness of Life requires the heart to open. To return to what was stated earlier: The opening of a human heart necessitates a reduction of fear. Much fear is based upon the human need to feel "superior" to others, including other life forms. If humans could understand that, *in the big picture, there are no life forms that are superior to others*, perhaps they would relax into being: Being the most joyful Beings they can Be.

The inner joy of being comes from an appreciation that *all Life is One, all Life is Good. All Life is To Be Respected.* All Life literally "runs" on the electromagnetic energy of **Love**. With this understanding, the human heart can embrace the concept of **Oneness** wholly.

❖

Arthur Fiedler

Wisdom from Beyond

Arthur Fiedler

Music is playful. Apart from the energy of the natural world, music is the most joyful vibration on Earth. It adds lightness and brightness to the physical plane. It sets toes tapping, hands clapping and, as performed in the manner I enjoyed most when conducting the *Boston Pops* in my incarnation as Arthur Fiedler, it brings smiles of delight and laughter.

Music abounds in the higher realms. We in Spirit can "tune in" to any composition we wish to hear. And, more, we can compose with an ease that would be the envy of Earth-based creators! Music is, as the saying goes, a gift of the gods, a blessing from Spirit.

Music is pure vibration, invisible, yet with the ability to move hearts mightily. Being simply vibration, music communicates to humans the truth: *Just because something cannot be seen doesn't mean it doesn't exist*. Everything on Earth, as quantum physicists are now confirming, is vibration. And, music is a great teacher of this.

Music is so powerful that humans should be careful as to which expressions of it they invite into their energy field. Music, if it channels purposes that are less than loving—even in churches or patriotic parades—can convert souls to causes that are not for the highest and best.

Mostly, music heals. Humans can serve themselves very lovingly by incorporating healing sound into their lives as much as possible. And, I remind all, music is portable. There's no need for the elaborate technological devices that humans use to hear *others* perform. *You* carry a musical

Arthur Fiedler

instrument with you wherever you go: *Your Voice*. **Use It!** If you feel you have been "judged" on Earth as not having a "good" voice, *rewrite* that message to yourself. Singing is a gift available to every human.

Because it opens humans' energy field, singing is healing. To double the healing power and joy, find a place of beauty and solitude in nature, and *sing your heart out—of sadness, into wholeness*.

Singing reminds me of a line from a song on earth plane:

"The best things in life are free."

❖

Wisdom from Beyond

Ella Fitzgerald

Singing is a gift from Spirit. It is one of the purest gifts that passes from the lighter vibration of the spiritual realm to the denser physical plane of Earth.

Singing is different than other musical vibrations on Earth in that the spiritual energy comes from a human's employment of its own physical instrument: the voice. Thus, singing brings the two realms, spiritual and physical, into a joint venture, for healing. And, it is this healing aspect that creates the joy singing gives humans.

The healing potential is why *every human is encouraged to sing*, no matter the qualities of an individual voice. Those humans who, for whatever reason, have taken on a belief that their voices are not "good enough" to be heard, even by their *own* ears, are allowing ego to seriously interfere with their adventure in awareness during incarnation.

Many on Earth have been led away from the glorious gift that singing is intended to be. It can be said to be no less than *tragic* when young humans are discouraged from singing by parents or peers. And, even more so by teachers too goal-oriented to encourage in each child its soulful desire to bring forth music with its own physical instrument. To give voice to its *own* voice is a joy every human deserves to experience—often.

In my incarnation as Ella Fitzgerald, I was blessed to be immersed in the joy of singing. As much as I delighted entertaining others with my voice, I was blessed beyond measure with being able, literally, to sing my way through the lessons that were a part of that life.

Ella Fitzgerald

Those who have a gift from the Creator to sing beautifully find great fulfillment in developing this talent. And, no doubt, bless others when sharing their gift. However, *all* humans have in their own throats the means to bless themselves. It is essential for humans to appreciate that singing—in the shower, while walking, bicycling, gardening, driving, alone or with others—is a practice to encourage in themselves.

Listening to others sing may be wonderful, but *singing oneself is to heal.* **Please**, *hark my message.* In singing, each of you brings harmony and wholeness to yourself, and joy and peace to the Universe.

SING, SING, SING!

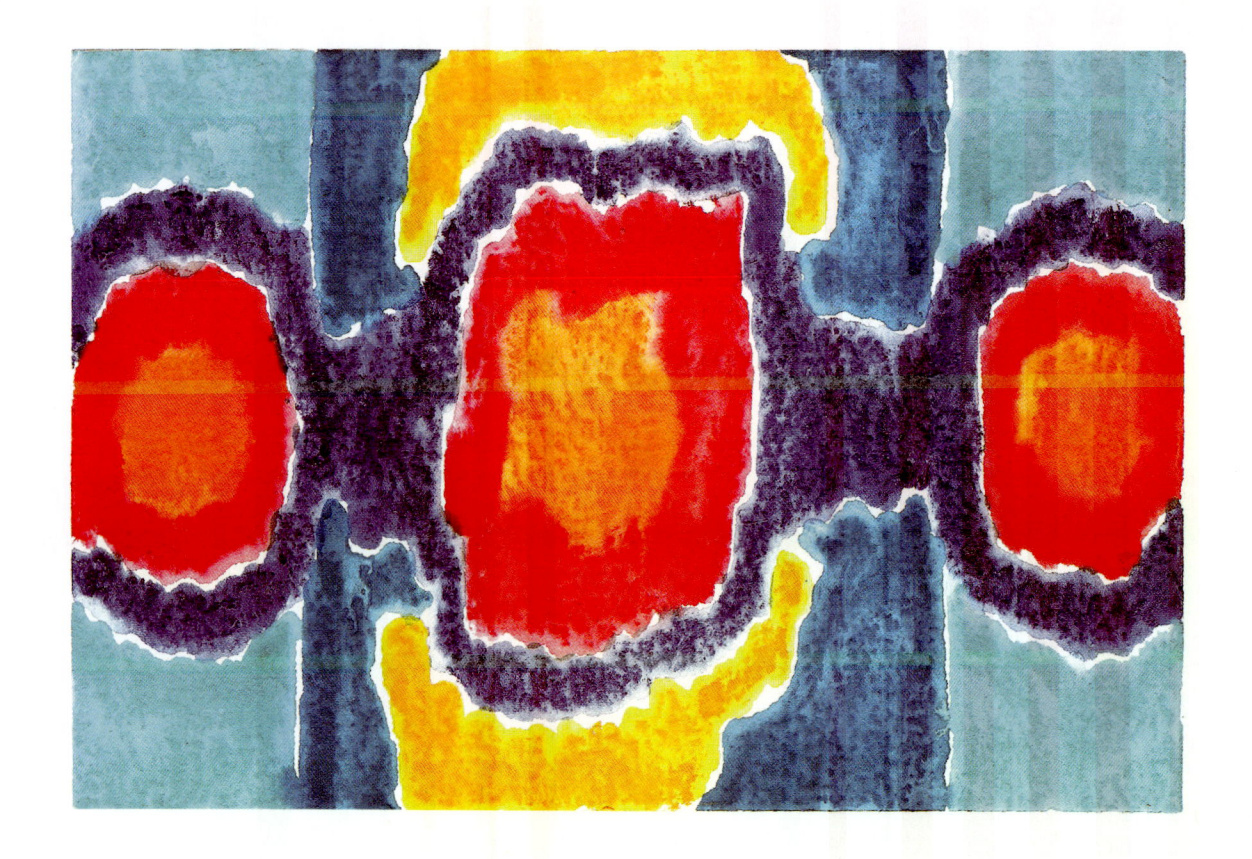

Samuel Clemens

Wisdom from Beyond

Samuel Clemens (Mark Twain)

Top of the day to you! I am so pleased for the opportunity to communicate across the energy from the spiritual to the physical realm. From my perspective I have much that I would share with humans on Earth today. For the present experience I will be concise.

The potential that is embodied in human existence is exceptional. It seems a great shame, from where I now reside, to note the great limits many humans accept in their vision of what is possible in life. Incarnated as Samuel Clemens, later known as Mark Twain, I lived quite expansively on Earth. I am coming through to say that *every* human has the choice to embrace dreams, to live into a larger experience than earthly circumstances might seem to indicate possible.

Every being is blessed with a spiritual essence that is its *True Self*. This Self has **no limits**. In physical existence, however, humans often do not recognize this spiritual aspect that makes them truly *unlimited*. As was the case in my life, often what are judged to be difficulties, even tragedies, on Earth are, in truth, opportunities.

As I see it, it is important for humans to surround themselves with energies, with influences, that are positive. Such "higher" energy opens them to their spiritual aspect. With this awareness, humans absolutely *can* break through the heaviness, the seeming restrictions, of physical existence that seem to limit what is possible. The truth that humans on Earth can know for themselves is that **Life is unlimited**.

Samuel Clemens

It also is true: whatever can be imagined can be manifested, on Earth as in Spirit. In the spiritual realm the reality is: Visualize, and the vision manifests. In the higher vibrations this process is natural, and virtually instantaneous. (This creates its own manner of learning, believe me!) In general, the lessons in Spirit are moved through more easily than they are on Earth because of the lightness of being here.

What I want to share with humankind is that the experience of life on Earth can be as "light" as an individual envisions. Eternal Life, including those portions of it in physical form, is intended to be lived ***LARGE***. Its learning is meant to come from exploring expansive paths rather than limited ones. When the "high road" energy is followed, it brings inner joy to earthly life. It creates what can be called "Heaven on Earth."

Thank you for continuing to read my words, now delivered from afar! ***PLEASE***, consider what I am sharing with you. Expand your beliefs about Life, in particular the portion you are experiencing ***NOW***.

❖

Wisdom from Beyond

Thomas Edison

I am the energy that incarnated on Earth as Thomas Edison. Electricity is a natural force on Earth, but harnessing it consciously to benefit humans was a concept I received intuitively in my physical life as Edison.

Prior to the invention of artificial light, the rhythm of life on Earth was ruled by the Sun. The hours of sunlight and darkness prescribed human activity. Lightness and darkness informed all aspects of life for all beings, especially humans.

Living in the rhythm of natural light connected all beings to Earth. Early humans led lives that required all their daylight hours and energy to be spent ensuring their continuing existence, by hunting and gathering for water, food, clothing, and shelter. As their lives eventually became less transient, humans became more reverential about the bounty provided for them by Earth. And, they recognized that they owed their very aliveness to the light of the Sun. They knew the Sun to be the supreme energy of their world.

Today, with the prevalence of artificial light on Earth, many humans have retreated from honoring the Sun in the way their predecessors did. Many do not appreciate the ultimate gift that sunlight is to their lives. The natural light of the Sun is necessary not only to sustain the body, but also to nourish the soul.

Of course, the accessibility of artificial light has been an important development for humans. Light becoming available through technology enabled humans to evolve in their creativity. There are more hours during which they can see to do the work their hearts and hands want to fashion.

Thomas Edison

It is important for humans to remember, however, that light is not mere technology. The Sun "blesses" Earth, enabling it to support Life. On Earth, **all** flows from and because of the Sun. Its light is sacred. If humans acknowledge this with gratitude, they will feel more connected to the natural world. This will affect, for the positive, the quality of their lives while incarnated.

Blessings from the Light in Spirit.

❖

Georgia O'Keeffe

Wisdom from Beyond

Georgia O'Keeffe

When my spirit was incarnated as Georgia O'Keeffe, I loved the Sun. I suppose I eventually lived in the desert southwest of the United States of America to experience the Sun more fully. I was attracted to the Sun's energy, of course, as are all humans, even if they are not consciously aware of their response to it.

Humans know they need the heat of the Sun in order for the Earth to be habitable. The Sun provides warmth for the growth of plants for food, keeps water in a liquid state to drink, and gives light to conduct daily activities by. Beyond these physical provisions, the Sun supplies spiritual energy. This energy is the essence of Life, the connection that each human has with the Universal Spirit/Creator. There is a spark of the Universal Spirit in each of us, and it is the Sun that keeps this spark energized.

The life-enhancing spiritual sustenance that the Sun provides can, perhaps, best be appreciated when observing humans who live in areas where sunshine is limited. In Earth's far northern latitudes, where the Sun shines for only a few hours a day in winter, humans experience a decided effect from the seasonal shift. As daylight in these regions decreases dramatically, many humans find themselves faltering in their ability to carry on daily life without spiritual support from the Sun. Reactions to their disconnection from the Sun's light in the darkest months can include increased rates of alcoholism, depression, suicide, and domestic violence.

Georgia O'Keeffe

Even when artificial light is available, it does not fully compensate for the reduction of sunlight in winter to support humans' inner sparks of Spirit. These may flicker fragilely in the earth plane's over-crowded, separated-from-nature, materialistic societies that today have a limited understanding of the importance of the Sun to the human Spirit.

The Universe has created a gift for humans, who have become increasingly separated from Earth's natural rhythm: Sunflowers. Sunflowers are one of the Sun's energetic representatives on Earth, and their beauty attracts humans to the positive energy they offer. The present popularity of Sunflowers is an inner response in humans for what their spirits know they need. It could even be said that Sunflowers are on a mission!

As humans become cognizant of their physical, mental, spiritual and emotional needs for Sun energy in its primary and secondary forms, they also will become more aware of the beautiful and intricate balance that enables Life to exist on Earth. Those of us in Spirit hope that the strains humans place upon Earth will be replaced with attitudes and acts of appreciation.

My spirit sends yours the power of a Sunflower.

❖

Wisdom from Beyond

Mary Baker Eddy

I am here to bring healing information to Earth. That was my life's work in the incarnation as Mary Baker Eddy. What a wonderful opportunity this connection affords to continue that education for humans.

There is no question that the natural state of the human form is wholeness. The Source of the Universe would not have created any state less than perfection. While the lower frequency of the energy vibration on Earth creates a challenge for humans, it also offers them opportunity to consciously coordinate mind, body, and Spirit, which is necessary in order to remain in the flow of wellness.

The emergence of quantum physics on Earth supports some of the concepts I sought to communicate to humans through the Christ, Scientist religion I developed during the Mary Baker Eddy lifetime. From the perspective in Spirit from which I am communicating now, however, I see that the challenge of any religion on Earth is that it eventually claims "followers," who are asked to practice faithfully the dictates of the one, or the few, who "lead" the organization. This is where all religions on Earth run into difficulties with what humans like to refer to as "*The Truth.*"

If you have been paying attention, you probably are aware that each of the world's major religions professes universal wisdom. Each, indeed, proclaims fragments of the truth, but none represents the whole of it. Depending upon how *attached* given religious administrations are

Mary Baker Eddy

to their particular brand of beliefs and practices, these can become the cause for serious feelings of separation between humans who follow different religious dogmas.

This sense of separation stems from a fear that if *others* are "allowed" to hold conflicting religious beliefs, one might not *oneself* be the "holder of absolute Truth." This fear taps into the deepest one of the human experience: *What happens at the end of a lifetime on Earth?*

Organized religions with highly-defined dogma are designed to hold systems of beliefs intact and unchanging. From the perspective I now have, I see that many religions are constructed less to encourage humans to open to their own understanding of the spiritual laws by which the Universe exists, than to keep them "captive" to an established ideology. I could go so far as to say that, for some religions on Earth, the purpose is to keep believers in "bondage" to an institutional mentality. This is a long way from supporting **each human being's right to the spiritual freedom to come to clarity from within its own soul as to what is the highest and best way to live**.

Guilt, shame, and all other feelings that can be traced back to fear, are among the tools used by some religious institutions to keep followers in tow to their version of "Truth." The desire to control other humans can lead to a greed for power, and for the money that seems to buy it. There is no automatic exception where religions are concerned.

What I observe from Spirit now is a gradual, very gradual, evolution on Earth to the realization that what would serve humankind best is that each being come to its own understanding—*from the inside out*—of principles for loving living. Rules imposed by others, *especially* spiritual ones, simply don't work.

Mary Baker Eddy

Each human is responsible for learning, through its life choices and experiences, what *rings true to the heart, not the mind*. The human heart is *not*—as the medical profession sees it—simply a physical organ. During physical life it is the casing for the soul, and when a human incarnation ends, the heart energy joyously reunites with the higher vibration of which it has always been a part.

I see such beauty and perfection in Creation with the larger view of Eternal Life from Spirit. I am grateful that I was able to advance a realization of the non-physical world while I was on Earth as Mary Baker Eddy. I close by saying:

As humans, you have nothing to fear
On Earth, or in Spirit.
All that needs to be attended to is.
Trust your heart to lead you toward the Loving Knowledge of Life.

❖

Liberace

I was a free spirit when incarnated on the earth plane as Liberace. In the spiritual realm, the true home of all beings, each soul knows it is free, with an understanding of freedom that is beyond the comprehension of those in physical life. My energy chose to come to Earth as Liberace to demonstrate the diversity of life-style choices available to humans. Each life on Earth has value, and humans are free to make widely varying choices as to what they wish to experience in a given incarnation.

In order to live a "good life" on Earth, it is not necessary to "do good," in the sense promoted by self-appointed human "do-gooders." When a soul in Spirit is making choices as to what to learn in its next physical life, there is no imperative about what the soul *should* select. The upcoming incarnation is for the evolution of that soul solely. There is only one overriding guideline as it sets its intentions for Earth: **Do No Harm.**

Having incorporated that edict into the experiences I set for myself in the Liberace lifetime, I determined to have fun, and to share it with others. A soul has the knowledge that there are many opportunities to incarnate in the physical realm and, thus, it can feel free to be playful in its choices. *Lightheartedness*, in fact, is one of the highest vibrations on the earth plane. To both be in lighthearted energy, and to share this state of being with others, is—contrary to many humans' conception of life—quite a "high" choice.

Liberace

Of course, once I was on Earth for awhile, I experienced the "forgetting" of the spiritual basis of life that is common for many humans. The physical world became the seeming substance of existence, and I forgot the laws of life that truly apply. Fortunately, the soul purpose I had set while in the higher vibrations "bled" through to my human self, and my heart claimed the lightness of being of Liberace. That *persona* was quite a character: "Over the top," I was called. I played out that incarnation in an openness of spirit, a sharing of fun, smiles, laughter, and the joy of music.

Despite my pleasure in the Liberace *persona*, many people judged it harshly. Now that my soul has returned to the perspective of the spiritual realm, I see that much of that judgment came from humans who felt burdened by the need to be serious about life, often far too serious. When such souls return to Spirit, they remember that there is no "extra credit" for those who live an overly-responsible life on Earth. Seriousness, in and of itself, is *not* a necessary lesson for any incarnation.

A human being living to "lighten up" itself, and to brighten up others, is more than sufficiently satisfying its soul goal. That intent does **No Harm** and, in truth, does **Much Good**.

❖

Martin Luther King, Jr.

Wisdom from Beyond

Martin Luther King, Jr.

W*hat the world needs now is **Love**.* I see from the perspective in Spirit that what humans need to learn most is that all the Universe is One. One energy: ***Love***. All consciousness is connected. No being, no life, is separated from any other. ***All truly are united in the living energy of Love***.

I had some sense of this in my earthly incarnation as Martin Luther King, Jr. But, I have grown in the knowledge of this truth since my return to the spiritual realm. I chose to incarnate on Earth in a time and place in which there was considerable separation, fear, even hatred, in order to learn more about ***Love***.

I was tested in my learning, as all humans are in their chosen lessons. The energy on Earth is so heavy and dense that it takes much effort to break through to seeing, feeling, and then being, an expression of Lightness.

It took a great deal of energy for me to continue learning these lessons on Earth. Nevertheless, I was convinced that the work I was engaged in, spreading the word about the need for all fellow beings to live lovingly with one another, was extremely valuable. Thus, I put my very soul into it.

Eventually, however, I became exhausted from the work: *Not* discouraged, just *so tired.* So, it was with mostly relief that I arrived at a doorway through which I could pass back to Spirit. The occasion of my "death" was only a seeming tragedy. The circumstances of a sudden death on Earth, even a violent one, have been self-sanctioned, at some level, by the soul involved

Martin Luther King, Jr.

while preparing its life incarnation plan. During the planning period, the soul is in the energy of Spirit, and well aware that Life is eternal and that there is *no death*.

Because of the chemistry of the physical Earth, humans can be quite slow to grow in awareness of spiritual truths. "Drama" can be a jump start to their growth. Often, as was the case in my passing, an opportunity to "cross over" is taken because the drama of its timing can add even more effect to the teachings being offered to those alive on Earth at that time. The drama causes humans to reflect more deeply on the issues involved than would otherwise be the case.

The Universe always is operating in the energy of **Love**. Guardian angels, healers, and helpers always are working with humans to help them learn what they chose to come to this incarnation for, and point the way to what will be most helpful for that learning to occur. This is always accomplished with **Love,** when seen from a higher perspective than is possible from the earthly plane.

The fact that Life is eternal is the greatest sign that the Universe is a loving place. If learning does not occur in one lifetime, there are as many opportunities to learn as one needs. No soul ever is "given up on." Each moves forward to success at the speed it has chosen.

Some lifetimes offer an opportunity for a quantum leap to more deeply identify with **Love**. This could be for one's own soul growth, and/or for others' growth, for the planet, even the Universe. Such was the experience in which I participated in my incarnation as Martin Luther King, Jr.

❖

Wisdom from Beyond

Vincent van Gogh

The aspect of my energy that sought to be a minister in the incarnation as Vincent van Gogh is especially grateful to be able to make this communication with humans on Earth now. There was a time in that Earth lifetime when I literally gave coal miners who were under my clerical care shirts off my back. I see from the perspective I have now in the higher vibrations that this is not necessarily the best way to help humans. It is when people learn to live from within themselves, to take responsibility for their actions, their thoughts, and their beliefs in life, that they realize the spiritual progress that they came to Earth to create.

The true learning that humans accomplish in earthly incarnations comes not from what they are given, but from that which they achieve through their own efforts. Those experiences may be "hard" or "soft," according to their understanding of how energy works.

I am here. I did not realize until recently that communication such as this was possible between the Spirit vibration and Earth. What a large canvas this presents for the transference of information that is important in Life!

From my perspective now, and as I review the experience I had in physical life while incarnated as Vincent van Gogh, I feel great compassion for all human beings. Every human is

Vincent van Gogh

doing the best it can with the awareness and understanding it presently has concerning Life. Many humans have occasional glimpses, inner flashes, of truth about eternal existence, but few are able to hold on to these pieces of soul knowledge. Fewer still can integrate them into their daily lives on Earth.

Although by virtue of having returned to the higher vibrations I am now removed from the incarnation as Vincent, I can summon the feelings I experienced during that existence. I often felt isolated, yet had a *knowing* that there was a connection to my soul to be reached, especially through the natural world.

As Vincent, I struggled spiritually, as all humans do at some level in every physical existence. Eventually, I came to an awareness that I had "done my work" for that lifetime. I did not commit suicide. The so-called "ear episode"—the result of a seizure—was an occurrence that created a pathway for me to depart from the physical realm and return to Spirit.

Instantaneously, I was joyful to be once again in the higher vibration, shed of the physical body. My soul is much greater than the energy that was called Vincent van Gogh on Earth. It continues to express itself in art, as it always has, long before the lifetime as Vincent.

Humans would serve themselves better if they were gentle with themselves. Although this is difficult in the density of the Earth energy, learning to become gentle with one's Self in physical life represents spiritual development. It requires a releasing of fear about the process of Life, and acquiring an understanding that *human beings are never alone. There are masters, teachers, guides, angels, and many other loving beings to assist in one's life learning. Listening from the soul for this help may be as important an accomplishment as a human can achieve on Earth.*

Vincent van Gogh

Being engaged in a creative process helps a human connect with its soul. Every human has creative energy, which expresses in the daily choices it constantly makes. Building in periods of solitude for reflection and meditation can increase awareness of this. A human's realization of its soul and the wonder of Life is the highest use of creativity.

❖

William James

I am truly pleased to be able to commune with you on the Earth plane today. It is an uncommon pleasure, to be sure, and I shall enjoy our exchange to the fullest measure.

Life on Earth is so very different from that in the realm of higher vibration, where souls spend the vast majority of eternal life. As a soul prepares itself to come to the Earth plane for an incarnation, there is much excitement among its fellow soul group members. Many of them will be joining in the incarnation "play," although some will have only "bit parts." Indeed, from the perspective of Spirit, an Earth life is somewhat like a theatrical production: stage, sets, props, and players, all gathered to create the life learning that has been scripted for the incarnation adventure.

There is, of course, free will on Earth. We philosophers who have incarnated there have weighed in on that subject endlessly over the centuries. Yes, there *is* free will for humans, but the parameters for a given life are set by the soul itself *before* its transition to Earth. A framework for a particular incarnation is provided, with advantages and adversities that can propel the soul towards the lessons it undertakes to master in that lifetime.

There is admiration from those in Spirit for those souls which opt for incarnations on Earth. Earth is known, one could say, as the Universe's "school of hardest knocks." It, indeed, *does* take courage for a soul to journey to the dense vibrational atmosphere on Earth, considerable

William James

courage. It's an exaggeration, perhaps, but one could say it's a bit like a sailor on an earthly pre-Columbian ocean voyage, a time when it wasn't at all certain that the ship might not fall off the edge of the world.

The "forgetting" of the truths of eternal Life in the spiritual realm that overtakes humans once they are on Earth is what makes physical life such a challenge. A soul, at the time it is incarnating, knows it will return to Spirit at the end of that lifetime. However, once in physical form, most humans eventually forget that knowledge.

A soul arriving from the spiritual realm duly enters its chosen human mother's womb and the actual fetus sometime reasonably close to physical birth. It then goes through what for it, now suddenly in physical form, is the fairly terrifying birth process. This process can be made less harrowing for newborns on Earth in some ways, but the shock for the incarnating babe is great no matter what, because of coming from a place of Light and Spirit to the physical world of flesh and gravity.

Many in Spirit serve a soul making this transition. These workers also may continue to help young humans remain in contact with their spirituality by serving as so-called "imaginary friends" or "angels" during their early Earth years. Thereafter, for most humans, the pull of gravity and the density of the vibration on Earth lead to a "forgetting" of most recollections of life in the Light—where souls are free of physical form, able to manifest and communicate by thought, and relocate at will.

William James

At present, more souls who will be able to continue to recall the truths of Life on the eternal spiritual plane are incarnating on Earth. Among these are the so-named *indigo children*, who are aware of the great transformation now coming to Earth, and who have signed on for special duty in its implementation. The earthly path is not necessarily easier for these souls, by any means, but they have offered this service to other humans as part of fulfilling their own life learning.

The present truly is a transformational time for Earth. There have been many other such ages, of course. My incarnation as William James took place during a time of great technological advancement for human society, with strides as well in the social and psychological sciences and philosophy.

My incarnation as William James encompassed a curious combination of science and spirituality. To become established in the academic exploration of the human mind and personality during the early days of social science, it was considered necessary to relegate such study to fairly rigid definitions, seeking to make human beings "objectified," rather than "free spirited"—as would better have been considered. And, thus, I established myself as one who dependably followed the scientific model for the study of human nature.

There came a time, however, when I was exposed to expanded ideas about reality. Such thinking created in me a sense of "remembering" spiritual concepts that I absolutely *knew* to be true, though many of them were scorned by the scientific community at my time on Earth. I had never intended, or imagined, to find myself outside the main stream of scientific thought, as I then did.

Nevertheless, I so resonated with my recollection of spiritual truths that I could not return to my previous way of thinking. The belief that Life was continuous, for example, and that one's current human span is only a limited experience in the vast expanse of existence, was thrilling, and felt deeply true to me. I found many such spiritual concepts to be confirmed by "happenings" and "coincidences" of which I became increasingly aware.

These new understandings made my life far more interesting and much more pleasurable to contemplate. There was no longer any need for a fear of death, since there was, as had been proven to *my* satisfaction, **no death** to be experienced at the end of this human lifetime, or any other that might follow. On Earth I found spiritual kinsmen with whom to share this thoroughly consuming knowledge. It completely changed my life to have opened to the awareness deep in my soul that there is no death.

I believe that this is the single greatest gift that I, or any other entity from the higher vibrations, can pass along to humans on Earth: ***There is no death***. There is simply the joyful passing to another form of existence: A return home, as it is often described, to the non-physical and very full life in Spirit.

My regret is that I was not more successful at being able to communicate this to others whilst I was on Earth as William James. Now, I have another opportunity to share this truth, and I see that the need for this information on Earth is greater than ever. I am grateful for the chance to offer this service.

Eleanor Roosevelt

Wisdom from Beyond

Eleanor Roosevelt

You, each one of you who is on Earth at present, are there at a time when you can make a great difference. Your thoughts and actions create an everlasting energy. Therefore, it is important, for the good of humankind, Earth, and the whole Universe, that you put out into the atmosphere the highest and best energy you are capable of producing with your current awareness and understanding of Life.

If you have the intention of living in the most conscious way you can, not only for your own well-being but for that of the world as well, you will find your life flowing more peacefully, harmoniously, and joyfully. If you will allow, *will encourage,* yourself to become more aware of your actions, *and reactions*, you will not only find yourself making positive change in your life, but enjoying the process as if playing a game.

Life, and how you live it, is a serious business. It, indeed, is important what energy you put forth into the world, because that energy lasts forever. However, the "lighter" your energy is as you choose the thoughts, words, and actions that moment-to-moment create your life, the more it will feel like play. Realize that living *light-heartedly* is an attitude that will bring about what is the wisest and best for you, as well as for the world.

❖

Frank Sinatra

Wisdom from Beyond

Frank Sinatra

All of us who have made the transition back to the higher vibrations of Spirit are grateful to be in the energy from which I am contacting you. However, we are greatly excited to know that communication with the physical sphere can continue. As the energy that incarnated on Earth as Frank Sinatra, I am thrilled to be able to connect with humans in this way.

Since Life is ongoing, it is important for beings on both sides of the "curtain" that *seems* to separate us to know that such valuable contact is possible. The difference between the vibrations on Earth and those in Spirit can be a challenge to overcome. The energies on both sides of the "veil" have to be willing to work at making the connection.

All energy is vibration. Since most humans readily understand that music is vibration, music can help them to comprehend the very foundation of the Universe. Music is used by those in Spirit to make contact with beings on Earth. Humans are more open to this knowledge about vibration when they hear music. This particular soul energy is now sending a serenade to you from the part of it that identified as Frank Sinatra.

A fragment of song that once was a mutual favorite of a human and a soul that now has passed back to Spirit, is one of the easiest connections that can be made between the physical and spiritual realms. So, be aware of the snatches of melody that float to you on Earth. When you hear one you respond to, know that a loving reach across the vibrational breach may be taking place.

❖

Fred Astaire

Wisdom from Beyond

Fred Astaire

I am dancing for JOY, as the energy that incarnated on Earth as Fred Astaire. The joy of movement was the greatest delight of my physical experience.

Movement in the gravitational force of Earth is entirely different from what it is in the spiritual realm. There, movement is accomplished by the mere thought of it. Although physical weightiness on the earth plane is challenging for humans, while dancing the body—briefly—can reach beyond the bonds of gravity. That's why my focus in the Astaire life was so satisfying!

Movement in all energy fields, especially the physical, creates positive feelings. The term "movement" implies reaching forward, which is why it feels good. Movement is change, which is always occurring in the Universe.

To *not move* results, energetically, in stagnation or retreat. Having no movement creates a feeling much like "blockage." In this situation, humans may develop feelings of unwellness or depression, especially if they actively "resist" movement or change. The underlying reason humans resist movement is fear: fear of the unknown.

The consequence of lack of movement is very predictable in humans. They lose flexibility and feel frustrated when it is restricted. However, even humans who live with great limitation in their physical mobility can learn to *move forward mentally*. In embracing that effort, often they can progress toward recovery of physical movement as well.

Fred Astaire

One of the main reasons for life experience on Earth is to learn *acceptance of change*. It is to realize, and accept, that every aspect of life is in a constant state of flux. It is to learn that *change is perfectly natural, in fact necessary, to Life*. Change balances all the various energetic forces that ebb and flow throughout existence.

Change in Life cannot be extinguished. Fear of change can be extinguished. Learn to move with change. Enjoy the movement.

Dance for JOY!

❖

Wisdom from Beyond

Mohandas Gandhi

D ear Ones: I am with you at this time, joyfully ready to speak to you from the higher vibrational realm where my soul now resides. This is a time of truly transformational change in the Universe, and it is on Earth that change will be experienced to the greatest degree.

There is no reason for anyone to be frightened about these changes. For, **all will be well. All is always well in Life, which is eternal.** Therefore, there is never any need to fear death, as so many humans do.

Yes, Life continues after the change that is called "death" on Earth. That change is, in fact, no more than an alteration in vibrational rate to a higher frequency that renders the physical body unnecessary. This leaves the newly transitioned soul relieved from the cumbersomeness of flesh, feeling the completely realized freedom that, in truth, it always has—even on Earth.

The joy that a being feels upon returning to Spirit is nearly indescribable. Life in the higher vibration is a wondrous state, which is inadequately but, perhaps, best expressed in the phrase *Lightness of Being.* Suffice it to say, the still-earthbound family members and friends of one who has crossed over would rejoice for their loved one if they knew the truth of that experience.

Of course, as humans, family and friends may grieve *for their own loss,* but they need never do so on behalf of the loved one returned to Spirit. As comfort, humans **can know** that reunion with loved ones awaits when they themselves move back to Spirit.

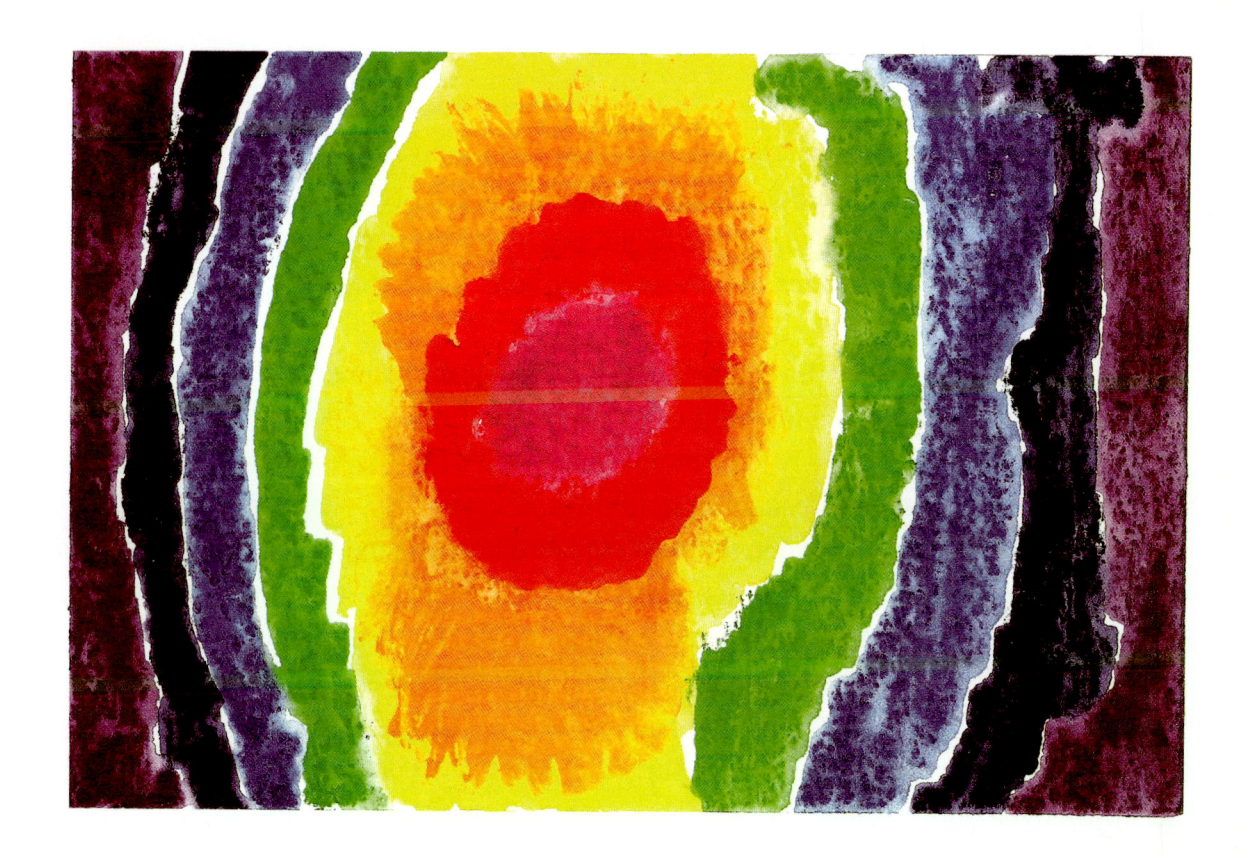

Mohandas Gandhi

I was not unaware of the truth of the soul's transitional journey when I was in human form as Mohandas Gandhi. Nor, was I unaware when the time for my own passing came, seemingly so suddenly and tragically. However, I *was unprepared* for the joy, beauty, and peace which greeted me in the Spirit realm immediately upon crossing over.

I had sought to live a "conscious" life in the incarnation as Gandhi. And, in that physical existence, I lived as much as I could in the present moment, not thinking ahead in anxious anticipation, or looking back upon past circumstances with regret. I did the best I could, from my understanding of existence during that life on Earth, to follow the path I gradually defined for myself.

From my vantage point now in the Spirit realm, I see that **all humans do the best they can with their present level of awareness.** And, I see that each human would be wise to accept that knowledge, with regard to itself, as well as others, rather than living in judgment.

A lack of judgment by humans for themselves, and for each other, brings an enormous benefit of peace to the Universe. To the extent that each is able, when humans embrace a large view of Life, granting forgiveness to those who cannot yet see so clearly, the spiritual service rendered by this effort is truly a gift to all of Life.

When I was on Earth as Gandhi, my human role grew to be a prominent one. I was in physical life at that time to be on a big stage, because human history was changing and new leadership was necessary. However, I can see now that peace can be propagated also on much smaller platforms, one person, one choice, at a time—with results that cumulatively result in

Mohandas Gandhi

life-transforming actions. Each human heart has the potential to greatly influence the energy on Earth, for the better, or not. *The raising of the collective vibration on Earth that transpires from each act of kindness, each effort to help a fellow being, does and will continue to provide for the common good.*

Do not let **seeming** tragedies discourage you. **From the earth plane, no one has the perspective to see the actual truth of events.** This is the case whether they be what are called—*most inappropriately*—"Acts of God," or are human-initiated unfoldments. *In the full picture,* every person, every being, is connected one to another. *Do Not Fear: Life is Good; Life is Eternal.*

And, may I say, do not rush your return to the spirit realm. Human life has many blessings and benefits that are not available in the higher vibrations. *Just know that when you are ready to make the transition back to Spirit, your soul will know. Then, you will be grateful for All that has been, and for All that is to be.*

I leave you in PEACE.

❖

/ Wisdom from Beyond

Robert F. Kennedy

To all beings who are presently living on earth plane, I can say that you have many opportunities for service at this moment. Shifts are taking place now in the vibrations in various realms of the Universe. Nowhere is this more true than on Earth.

From my perspective now, returned to Spirit following incarnation on Earth as Robert F. Kennedy, I take note of the high degree of fear that change often brings forth in humans. Change is always occurring in Life. Therefore, humans are well served to make peace with that fact, rather than ravaging their sensitive body forms with the emotional terrorism that fear produces.

I do not speak of fear as "emotional terrorism" lightly. The way the human mind operates, all the negative emotion that fear encompasses can make the hormonal system run wild, creating toxicity in the physical body. Fear produces even more toxicity than environmental pollutants, which are, quite rightly, of great concern on Earth now.

The human body, which lovingly encases the eternal soul during an earthly incarnation, is a very special organism. It is both more sensitive, and more self-sustaining, than most earthlings, including medical professionals, are aware. The human body is so carefully calibrated for self-healing that any correction for conditions that exist on the earth plane, even those due to foreign substances entering the body, should be undertaken only with great judiciousness.

I am choosing to speak of this matter, above all other knowledge I might have communicated back to Earth at this time, because I see the inner violence that is being perpetuated on the human body. This is especially true for native peoples, whose traditions

Robert F. Kennedy

and wisdom have virtually disappeared from Earth. This reduces the hope for world peace—which is related to wellness— at least until it is recognized how deeply the human condition has been affected. Earth is, indeed, an increasingly "small planet." As a result of technology, human patterns of action and reaction now spread rapidly around the globe. Some of these are decidedly not for the well-being of physical beings.

    I am aware that others in Spirit also have communicated, as I am doing here, to bring knowledge to humans to help defuse the deep fear of "death" that exists on Earth. The knowledge that *there is no death* is being brought forth from Spirit in many forms. Such communication is vital, for *if the fear of death could be removed from the human mind, freedom from that terrorism alone would make the human life experience a completely different one.*

    For those currently in the heavy vibrations on Earth, it may hardly be possible to realize how a major reduction in humans' fear of death, and the rise in vibration that would result from that, could completely transform life for all beings. Therefore, communicating that there is no such thing as death, in the way humans believe it to be, is a starting point for changing Earth.

    All the efforts humans now are engaged in with regard to respecting and restoring the Earth itself are excellent, and necessary. These efforts will automatically be strengthened once the fear that humans experience, because of their misperception of what occurs at the end of an earthly incarnation, has been eliminated.

    Once the great fear "death" is reduced, all related fears—especially the belief that there is not enough for everyone on Earth of the basics such as water, clean air, food and fuel—also will lessen. Then, life on Earth will be cooperative rather than competitive. ❖

Jesse James

Jesse James

I, the energy that was Jesse James on the earth plane, am here with a message for humans now incarnated. It is that the *very* independent behavior I exhibited in physical life, and the disregarding of other beings' rights to a safe and peaceful existence, never was, and *certainly is not now, acceptable*. The needs of Earth herself, and the population as a whole, require cooperation among humans around the planet as never before. The days when individuals could live in complete self-interest are past, even on the frontier.

This is not to say that individualism, in the form of free thinking, is not needed. Today, clear, independent thinking is essential on Earth. Such individualism, however, needs to be in the context of consideration for the higher good for all.

Ruthless and *mindless* actions—and it may surprise humans to realize that these words describe many actions which, *by the book*, are lawful—can no longer be absorbed by society. All actions must be considered thoughtfully by humans, who need to adopt their own internal sense of ethics and loving behavior for interacting with others in community. This is true for individuals, corporations (including institutional religions), and countries.

There now is a shift in energy upon Earth that requires all humans to be responsible for their own actions, *and their own thoughts*. They must recognize the need to connect harmoniously with the whole of society. There will no longer to be a "free ride," as they say on Earth, for those in positions of power and privilege.

Jesse James

This shift should not be a cause for fear. As has been stated by others, there are enough resources, including Love, to minister to all on Earth in abundance. But the "Robin Hoods" must now step forward, *lawfully,* to redistribute to *all* on Earth. In doing this, *humans will learn that there truly is enough for all. And that, therefore, there is no need to steal from others, or to hoard.*

Earth is abundant enough to provide a prosperous living for all humans. If change to this understanding is not participated in willingly and voluntarily, shifts *must* occur to bring about the necessary adjustments. It is Time.

❖

Wisdom from Beyond

Mary Cassatt

I am delighted to be able to speak to those on the earth plane in this way. Such a creative means of communication! When I incarnated as Mary Cassatt, Earth was largely a man's world artistically. My creative energies propelled me to follow my interest in drawing and painting from an early age. I was blessed by the strength of this desire to follow my joy, almost to the point of ignoring the social structure then prevalent both in America and on the European continent.

It is such a blessing to be guided to the inner feelings that energize one's being, that fulfill one's soul longings. Attending to these feelings is what leads to soul's work and joy. And this is what gives life its potential, the gift of what brings the highest good both for one's self and others.

A human rarely sees the whole of life's purpose and process clearly. There are many patterns that play out in any single lifetime, many forms of learning that accumulate as one advances through a given incarnation on Earth. What I learned as Mary Cassatt is that it is not selfish for humans to follow their deepest desires. It is these inner longings that enable the personality to take direction from its soul. It is these longings that indicate what the individual has chosen to come into human form to learn.

On Earth, much attention is paid to admonishments not to be selfish. Many religions pass judgment on humans' self-fulfilling actions as selfish, rather than the self-loving choices many

Mary Cassatt

of them are. Humans repeatedly are told: It is better to give than to receive. The way this usually is presented, however, is a distortion of the heart of this spiritual law, which is about balance.

Exchanges of giving and receiving need to flow in a circle. *Giving cannot take place if no one is willing to receive.* There must be a balance of giving and receiving. And, with this understanding, it becomes as sacred to receive as it is to give.

The so-called Golden Rule, "Do unto others as you would have them do unto you," is a core concept of every major religion on Earth. Many, however, put doing for others ahead of, or instead of, honoring oneself. It is not a matter of "either/or," but a balance of both. When one feeds oneself on loving kindness, forgiveness, and compassion, these qualities are then abundantly available from within to give to others. Learning this during my incarnation as Mary Cassatt gave me the loving energy to care for family members and others, while maintaining the strength to pursue my creative work.

The energy I worked with as an artist in the incarnation as Mary Cassatt was very loving, very comforting. I suppose this was why my subject matter so often involved domestic scenes, especially women and children. Although I had no children of my own in that lifetime, I was not

Mary Cassatt

lonely or unfulfilled. My spirit had had other incarnations on Earth in which I had been either mother or father. As a result of sensing that, I was able to release the need to have a child as Mary Cassatt. Also, I had learned by that lifetime that there are many satisfying ways to bring children into one's life on Earth, not merely by giving physical birth to them.

My principle creative energy as Mary Cassatt went into my art. Humans have to make choices as to what they focus upon. There are those who speak of "having it all" on Earth. In truth, however, humans find the deepest satisfaction when they move more deeply into a select few endeavors. To gain the most fulfillment from a given lifetime, a human needs to achieve a balance between the breadth and depth of its interests and goals. This is not a balance that comes from the human mind, but one found in the heart. By following one's heart, a human is guided to the lifetime intentions its soul has set.

Always, it is a matter of balance. A reckless pursuit of "happiness" may lead to consequences that are very much less than happy. Should this occur, however, the choices that led to it are not necessarily to be regarded as mistakes. Human life, with its gift of free choice, is meant for learning. When balance eventually is chosen, and awareness is gained, inner joy prevails.

We in Spirit want to communicate to those on Earth that the sense of "family" in the Universe is much more expansive than it generally is considered to be by humans. *All life is family.* Every natural thing is living and has a connection to the energy of every other living thing. Ants and eagles; rocks and raccoons; free-ranging animals, domesticated pets; people from all races, regions, and religions. And, the Earth/*Gaia*, which embodies the loving energy that cares for this physical family, is a super matriarch, we could say. The more that humans open their hearts to this larger sense of "family," the more peaceful life on the planet will be.

There is new energy coming to Earth at this time. It is encouraging humans to move toward embracing this greater understanding of the connectedness of all Life. It is the responsibility of humans to attend to creating health and harmony on their own planet, *before* connecting with other worlds. Many of the vibrations currently present on Earth do not resonate with the rest of the Universe.

Life forms from other worlds are well aware of the state of being on Earth. Many of these so-called "extra-terrestrials" are more advanced in their mode of existence than humans. In fact, they have been helping human civilization in many areas, for many eras. These beings a have much higher intention for good than has been portrayed on Earth.

To return to what is True: All Life is One, One for Good. As humans grow in this understanding, the Earth itself will shift to greater harmony.

❖

Dag Hammarskjöld

Wisdom from Beyond

Dag Hammarskjöld

*E*very human is a being of beauty and love. And, it is no exaggeration to say that each human is an essential portion of the whole of the Universe. Therefore, the wars, jealousies, and all the power struggles that result from *the fear one human has of not being as "valuable" as another person*, **must cease.** It is essential for Earth at this time to be a more united place for humanity.

When I was incarnated on Earth as Dag Hammarskjöld, I served the United Nations organization. The United Nations sought, and still seeks, to establish that respect for the self-determination of all humans is more important than national origin, race, or creed concerns.

The formation of the United Nations was a major movement forward for humankind, and it continues to serve as a shining model for the future evolution of humanity. Yet, it is worth remembering that no institution on Earth, whether political, religious, cultural, or other, can be perfect. This is because the humans who are instrumental in the organization and operation of such institutions are just that: **human.**

Nevertheless, the energy that is released into the world by the intention of humans to establish the highest international awareness and examples for all Life is **enormous.** This energy contributes to the evolution of every human's essential being, or soul. For those humans who can already hold a higher view for life on Earth, they *know* the Truth of which I speak.

Not all humans are yet actively engaged with the United Nations, or related non-nationalistic organizations. However, every positive thought, word, and deed that each

Dag Hammarskjöld

person contributes to the world, every day, adds *Love*, the powerful form of energy that moves all Life forward on its great journey. I repeat: **Each thought, each word, each action of each human increases—or does not—the amount of Love present on planet Earth, and throughout the Universe.**

Imagine what the change in energy would feel like if large numbers of humans become consciously committed to following this intention. The cumulative effect, the collective energy raised, would create a *fearless, joyful* environment that all beings could embrace.

From my perspective in Spirit, I see: *This Can Be Done. It Will Be Done. You can choose to begin your part now.*

❖

Wisdom from Beyond

Winston Churchill

One day on Earth I became aware of Life as being "larger" than I had ever imagined it before. In the mature period of my human incarnation as Winston Churchill, I knew myself to be a figure that was sometimes referred to as "larger than life." However, once I gained an awareness it is *Life itself*—that is, the energy which supports all Creation—that is large, I regarded myself and my fellow humans from a very altered perspective. It is Life, and all the energy that that implies, which propels us, each individual being, through the process of learning the marvelous truth of how magnificent existence *is*.

After I had this awareness, I may not have seemed to other humans to have changed so remarkably in outward appearance or behavior as Winston Churchill. But, within, I was completely transformed in the way I viewed my purpose for living.

This transformation, which came to me one day as I was immersed in the joy of painting a landscape, included a deep *knowing* that Life is continuous for all beings. I *knew* there is no death, as humans think of it. There is simply an eternal progression of experiences, in different energy environments, that each lead us toward greater awareness. And, with that awareness, to greater joy and peace, a greater sense of Love.

In the period on Earth in which I had this transformation, I found it difficult to communicate to others my experience of this expanded knowledge of the truth of human existence. At that time, many humans were embroiled in momentous armed conflict that encircled the Earth. The

Winston Churchill

energy created by conquering, killing, and controlling others—no matter which side of the conflagration one had allegiance to—was filled with fear, as war, and indeed all conflict, always is. Within the "theaters of war"—what a strange, or, perhaps, strangely appropriate name for the areas of conflict—there were expressions of authentic loving energy on the part of many individuals. But, overall, the energy on Earth during what is designated the first half of the Twentieth Century was predominated by aspects of fear.

What allowed humankind to avoid completely consuming itself in the tumultuous destruction then—and to this day—are the random expressions of **Love** that always are present in human souls. On Earth, as everywhere in the Universe, *the energy of Love is so much more powerful than that of fear that there never can be any doubt as to the ultimate outcome.*

And, so, human life *will* continue. *It will.* Humans are, in this present moment, mutating, changing, to be able to handle the higher vibrations of the increased **Love** which now is coming to Earth. This is a very positive mutation that is raising the vibration of Earth itself, and every being which has chosen to be on the planet at this time. From my perspective in the spiritual realm, I can see what a positive evolution this is.

Those who are residing on Earth at present have the benefit of living there at a time when the vibrational energy is rising. This will aid all humans in becoming aware, with new clarity, of

Winston Churchill

concepts of living in community more lovingly and cooperatively. Many, though not all, on Earth will elevate their awareness of the interconnectedness of Life. They will be able to shed the fears that have prevented them from realizing this before.

The change in vibration for Earth—*Good Vibrations!*—will take place over an extended period. As humans find themselves learning new ways to think, act, and interact, they will find themselves blessed with more peace and greater joy. ***Change for good is always coming to Earth, and now is the time for humans to know this.***

ALL IS WELL WITH THE WORLD.

Wisdom from Beyond

Anne Frank

I am here. I AM HERE. I will give my answer to your question. When, during my Earth life, I wrote the entries that later became *The Diary of Anne Frank,* I could never have imagined the journey that journal would have. It was no accident that my writings survived, of course, since I know now from my perspective in the higher realm that my *Diary* and life were meant to show the indomitable eternal spirit that is embodied in each human.

There is poignancy in the human condition during events such as war that happen in the course of life's lessons. These lessons, so challenging to master in the earthly realm, are simply second—no. *first*—nature when a soul returns to the higher vibrations of Spirit.

Once the conflagration that you know as the Second World War began during my Earth incarnation as Anne Frank, I felt protected as a young person from many of the fears that older humans had as they saw Society, as they had known it, radically altered by the political philosophy of a small group of people, the Nazis. Young humans, having arrived on Earth more recently from Spirit than the adults around them, carry a higher vibration that can counteract earthly conditions.

As Anne Frank, I had hopes for my future in that lifetime. But, I also lived very much in the present, accepting experiences as they came, moment to moment. As I look back from Spirit upon that life, hiding from the Nazis in an attic in Amsterdam with my family, I see that what enabled me to exhibit the emotional and spiritual strength I did was my ability to live in the present moment. Not looking back with regret, nor ahead with fear, during those many months.

Anne Frank

Few sharing the circumstances I was in at that time imagined what lay ahead for them. But the adults lived with a far greater sense of anxiety than the young. From my perspective now, I can see the value of the hope that the young people reflected back to the older humans around them.

This is Anne. A lesson I learned on Earth is one all souls need to absorb. Physical life is a treat, even with its lessons; but, it is a temporary one. *The deepest joy of existence is experienced in the eternal life of Spirit.* This knowledge is of great value for those now in human incarnation, as it will allow them to move beyond what may appear, on the physical plane, to be catastrophes. Since there is no death, not in Eternal Life, any transition back to Spirit is a perfectly natural occurrence, whenever and however it takes place for a human. In fact, the transition has been planned by the person's soul itself.

A departed soul's loved ones who yet live on Earth also have participated in the "plan." It calls for them to *know that they will be reunited in Spirit with their dear one. And, in the meantime, to move forward on their own soul goals in what remains of the Earth life for them.* This is the message that those who have passed to Spirit would most wish to offer across the realms to loved ones on Earth.

Anne Frank

From a perspective in the true home of Eternal Life, existence is a gentle, meaningful, flowing pattern in which a soul gradually grows in wisdom. Dear Ones, those who share a soul group and come together repeatedly for chosen learning adventures in various environments, *always* return safely *home to Spirit.* The truth is, there aren't any tragedies, only Life playing itself out.

Eternal Life, all of it, is a gift. If you can absorb this wisdom, you will shed fear, the great stumbling block of the physical realm. You will be able to appreciate every experience of existence for what it is: JOY.

I wish you to know this.

❖

Wisdom from Beyond

John Lennon

"You may say I'm a dreamer, but I'm not the only one." That was true when I wrote the lyric, and is even more true today, I am delighted to be able to observe from my perspective in the spiritual realm.

Many ideas for the harmonious existence of humans were given in song lyrics when I was on Earth in the incarnation of John Lennon. The energy which was imbedded in such songs still flows out in a ripple effect of peace whenever one is sung by a human or, even more so, by a group.

The energy of fear that is present on planet Earth is strong and infectious. However, it is not nearly as strong and infectious as the energy of Love. *"Love. Love, Love. Love is all we need."*

Love can solve all the seeming problems humans experience, *and* all the fears they have in anticipation of what *might* happen. In each *present moment*, a human is always able to choose to live with *Love.*

This is the energy of John. I see peace as an increasing possibility on Earth. This is because there are so many efforts on the part of so many—both on Earth and in Spirit—being made to raise the vibration on the planet.

John Lennon

There are those who will ask, "How can this be?" in the face of seemingly harrowing situations on the physical plane. However, from my perspective, I can *see* that the energy of Earth is evolving. **Alleluia!**

So many souls in Spirit and on Earth at this time have been preparing for this present moment for eons. And, now, the time is ripe. Shifts and adjustments are being accomplished to effect the changes that are coming. And, humans should know, **all is for the good.**

Never fear: This is a loving Universe. Be joyfully encouraged that every single effort each of you makes to think, speak, and act in ways that are for the highest and best for all, truly does benefit the whole of Life.

We in Spirit thank each of you on Earth for enthusiastically being the best you can be at this present time. You, and the Universe, will be blessed by your efforts. And, you will find ever increasing Joy, Peace, and Abundance.

❖

Michael Jackson

Wisdom from Beyond

Michael Jackson

I AM ALIVE! Passing over was easier than I imagined. And, now I can truly heal from the wounds I took on in the earthly incarnation as Michael Jackson.

There is much help for healing in the realm of Spirit, where *Unconditional Love* is ever present. My transition back to Spirit was not premature. The energy for that earthly existence had run its course. In Spirit I no longer have to struggle. I am very grateful to have returned.

As I return to a healed state, pain-free in the pure love present in the higher vibrations, I will be guided as to how to best serve humankind, how to add my energy to the constant stream of **Love** that constantly is being transmitted to Earth. If you get in touch with your eternal Self by becoming quiet, you will feel the Love; each of you will. Love is all the medication you need to heal any kind of pain.

You *can* heal your wounds while on Earth. The help of Spirit is all around you. Ask for it. Set your intention to *Be Healed Now*. Pain, either physical or psychological, is not necessary in Life. *Choose Wholeness—Right Where You Are Now*.

I LOVE YOU.

❖

Elvis Presley

Elvis Presley

When I survey Earth from my perspective in the higher vibration, I am amazed at the variety of lives humans create for themselves. All it takes is *imagination*, and then *intention followed by action*, in order to manifest what they desire. This is true for all humans, which is why the limitations of poverty or other physical circumstances are no deterrent once the imagination is engaged.

I had no particular social or economic advantages as a youth in my human incarnation as Elvis Presley. I *did* have a love of singing and an ear for music. Those gifts, and my mother's loving encouragement, sustained and nurtured me until I created with my imagination the opportunities that moved me forward.

For some musicians, what they have come to Earth to learn in a given lifetime is closely connected to "coming into their own" as entertainers. For me, there were, as well, other essential lessons to be learned. As Elvis, I had a "soul cushion" in the joy that making music provided me when some of my life's lessons—due to the freewill choices I made—challenged me greatly. In particular, these concerned psychological and substance abuse.

Eventually, I progressed enough to enable myself to return to the Spirit realm, for the rest, recovery, and rehabilitation that await all who need it after passing home. **Love** is always available to every soul, no matter the circumstance through which their earthly choices have led them. When returned to Spirit following an earthly incarnation, a soul quickly recalls the truth of existence: *Nothing matters except being in loving relationship with all of Life.*

Elvis Presley

There are wonderful pleasures of the senses on Earth for humans to experience. Enjoyed in the correct balance, these can add greatly to the happiness of physical life. However, the pure and deep joy of Life for which all souls yearn often comes from a greater understanding than most humans can retain. The point I want to offer here is that there is no need for guilt as to how we live an earthly existence. We always learn from our experiences. And, we always, indeed we must, have an opportunity to try again if we don't get a lesson mastered in any one incarnation.

There should be no guilt for your efforts on Earth, no matter how they turn out. This is not to say that humans shouldn't try to do the best they can in an earthly incarnation. Truly, though, they always are doing that: *The best they can with the understanding of Life that they have at their point of soul evolution*. What a gift the knowledge I am passing on to humans here is: ***No Guilt. Less Stress, More Joy.***

Live in the present moment. You can't go wrong in the present moment. The present moment is where you can sing your soul's music, which, as with everything your soul learns during its lives on Earth, stays with you when you return to the eternal realm. ***That soul learning is the mined gold which, when you pass on, is all you carry from Earth back to Spirit.***

❖

Wisdom from Beyond

Elizabeth Kübler-Ross

When I was on the earth plane incarnated as Elizabeth Kübler-Ross, I became associated professionally with the passage that humans call "death." I wrote particularly about the stages that human minds and hearts move through in accepting the passing on of their loved ones. Now, from a perspective myself in the Spirit realm, I would like to expand on this for those on Earth, where, for so many, their greatest fear is death.

The basic fact is: ***There is no death.*** When passing on from a life on Earth back to the realm of Spirit, a soul simply raises its vibration, which releases its connection to the physical body. The higher vibration renders the soul invisible to human eyes, which normally perceive only a quite limited range of vibrations. Other Earth forms, such as some animals, sense and see the higher vibrations of which I speak.

A being who has returned to the Spirit vibration hasn't really gone anywhere, certainly not "up" or "down." This is why humans, who are attentive and open to such experiences, might sense—from a breeze near them, the flicker of electric lights, or in faint strains of a memorable song—the presence of a loved one who has passed over. When a soul transitions from Earth back to Spirit in a state of acceptance, it usually will be available to its loved ones on the physical plane with supportive energy. All this is to say that those who have transitioned back to life in Spirit are near, and can send love and aid as requested in your thoughts.

While the energy of a soul that has passed on may remain around its still-physical dear ones for a while following its transition, eventually it will want to give attention to the reality and

Elizabeth Kübler-Ross

joys of ongoing existence in Spirit. It will hope that you can accept the change that has come for it: the joyful return home. It hopes you will continue with your Earth life of learning and loving.

Being aware of an ongoing connection with a soul who has passed on offers the potential of great learning for humans. A person yet remaining in physical form can ease into surrendering to what is, to the realization that its life also will eventually transition to Spirit. This will occur with a simple shift in vibration: no distress or pain, only joy. With this knowledge, the period between the transition of a dear one and your own, can be free from fear of passing on.

Life is for living as joyfully as possible. This is understood by souls in the Spirit realm, although humans on Earth may need to be reminded this is so. I speak not of a shallow human experience of happiness, but of the deep inner joy that humans feel in their hearts when experiencing what they incarnated on Earth to do.

The most loving way to honor your dear ones who have returned to Spirit is to accept this wonderful knowledge of what Life truly is. Continue to live fully in the present moment, enjoying the unique gifts of human existence, until your soul is ready to return to the even greater joy of Spirit.

There is no death. You will be with your loved ones again.
May you relax in the knowledge of this truth.

Afterword

In reading *Wisdom From Beyond* we have been introduced to a new perspective on Life. Reflecting on the messages will help move us from the prevailing fear that exists on Earth today to the ability to experience the love that exists all around us. Instead of finding ourselves with feelings of hopelessness, sadness, terror, and anger, due to behaviors and values expressed in the world, the entities are making us aware that change on a global level begins with choices we make on a very personal level. By placing ourselves in the loving energy of their healing messages, we become able to see those choices for change.

Gandhi's message proclaims: "All humans do the best they can with their present level of awareness." Since the entities' messages come from a higher energy field than Earth's, awareness expands from our very first reading of them.

While reading, take note of the messages that hold the most interest for you. This feeling of connection is how you are led to the wisdom you are ready to integrate. By returning to the messages and Soul Portraits that resonate with you, they become increasingly meaningful. As our understanding shifts, we may begin to relate to other messages that, on first reading, may not have "spoken" to us.

The entities will guide you, sometimes quite directly. You may find (as I do regularly) that you "hear from" one of the entities, through a strain of music, a work of art, a reference to it in a book or newspaper, on radio, TV, or the internet. This might be a suggestion that you could benefit from reading its message once again.

Afterword

We also can receive the entities' guidance by opening *Wisdom From Beyond*, seemingly at random. In doing this, you may find you have been inspired to turn to information that can be used in your life right in this moment. Allowing the entities to connect with us in any way they find possible increases our trust in the fact that ours is a loving Universe, which provides what we need exactly when we need it.

With Gratitude

I am grateful to the entities for the healing content of their communications in *Wisdom From Beyond*. And, for the awareness of our ongoing relationship with them and others in Spirit.

Many encouraged me as I sought to follow faithfully the inspiration that has brought this book into being. My appreciation to them all and, in particular, to Sondra Adelman, Elizabeth Anderson, Margaret Cristiano, Elizabeth Eldridge, Judith Fairbrother, Elaine Heller, Christopher Hill, Anne McNamara, John Rittell, Grazia Tomasello, and the Swampscott Church of Spiritualism (MA, USA) community.

At every stage, as *Wisdom From Beyond* became ready for its next step, souls arrived in synchronicity to provide all the resources needed. Just days after the entities first contacted me, Christina Cross appeared with her loving counsel. Thereafter, I was guided from one new supporter to another: Linda DeHart, Bill Kennedy, Patti Jones, Jane Berman, Pamela Marin-Kingsley, Denise Delaney, Norma Sellier. And, then, to Ted Poppe and Victoria Poppe. My thanks and blessings to you.

H. Constance Hill

About the Author

H. Constance Hill has been an independent journalist and author since 1980. She has lived in England and in Holland, and for many years specialized in travel writing, journeying globally. These experiences changed her world perspective from national to international.

Travel in the physical world nourished Connie's spiritual journey. She has studied widely in the metaphysical field, and continues to be both student and teacher of personal awareness workshops. Connie has uniquely combined her communications and artistic talents since she began channeling more than 10 years ago. As her work with Spirit evolves, she regularly receives wisdom from beyond, and guidance as to how best to serve as a spokesperson of integrity for it.

JONESIN' FOR A BOSS CHICK

A Montgomery Love Story

TN Jones

Jonesin' For A Boss Chick: A Montgomery Love Story

Jonesin' For A Boss Chick: A Montgomery Love Story © 2018 by TN Jones.

Published by Tyanna Presents.

All rights reserved. No part of this book may be reproduced in any form or by any electronic or mechanical means including information storage and retrieval systems, without permission in writing from the author. The only exception is by a reviewer, who may quote short excerpts in a review.

This book is a work of fiction. Names, characters, places, and incidents either are products of the author's imagination or are used fictitiously. Any resemblance to actual persons, living or dead, events, or locales is entirely coincidental.

Acknowledgment

First, thanks must go out to the Higher Being for providing me with a sound body and mind; in addition to having the natural talent of writing and blessing me with the ability to tap into such an amazing part of life. Second, thanks most definitely go out to my Princess. Third, Jammie Knight, Tyanna Coston, Tyanna Presents, Sunny Giovanni, Crystal Lett, Ke'Lena Wallace, Shanice Bryant, and Vanice McCullum where would a sister be without y'all. Fourth, to my supporters who has been rocking with me from day one, and to new readers for giving me a chance.

Truth be told, I wouldn't have made it this far without anyone. I truly thank everyone for rocking with me. MUAH! Y'all make this writing journey enjoyable! I would like to thank everyone from the bottom of my heart for always rocking with the novelist kid from Alabama, no matter what I drop. Y'all have once again trusted me to provide y'all with quality entertainment.

I hope y'all enjoy, my loves! (Muah.)

Jonesin' For A Boss Chick: A Montgomery Love Story

CHAPTER ONE
Madison 'Polo' Willis

Friday, May 25th, 2018

"It's officially summertime. The hoes gon' be half-naked an' ready to trip, split, fuss, an' fight over som' dick. I'on know 'bout y'all but I wanna see som' hoes show their asses 'bout my dick," Ponytail stated as I glared at him as if he had lost his mind.

"Dude, I swear you be actin' like you's a young nigga," Big stated before pulling on the fatty of a blunt he had rolled.

As they went back and forth, my cell phone dinged. Retrieving my phone from the holster on my pants, I shook my head at the niggas that had the same DNA code as me. I wasn't going to add my five cents to their conversation. They already knew how I rolled. I wasn't up for the bullshit. Off the rip, bitches knew that I wasn't the settling down type. I had that shit written all over my face.

Joana: My period off. Come through, quick fast and in a hurry.

That was the best text she could have ever sent a nigga. It had been six days since I had been in her guts. Hopping to my feet, I replied to the broad that had been a nigga's main piece of pussy for a year.

Me: *Aye, Ma, I'll hit you up when I'm on the way. At the garage.*

Three seconds later, she replied: *Okay.*

Sticking my phone into the holster, I waltzed off from the instigating and bickering niggas that I would kill over.

"Oh, so you ain't got shit to say, Polo," Dame laughed.

"Not a single thang," I replied as I stood in front of a newly painted rose gold, 1979 Buick Regal.

"So, what do you have planned fo' the summer wit' the hoes?" Russ asked as he stood in front of the car that was assigned to me.

"Shid, the same as I have planned fo' them year' round ... fuckin' them when I want an' actin like I don't know them when I don't want to be bothered wit'. I'm not the nigga fo' a relationship. That shit been sunk," I answered as my phone rang.

Instantly, I knew who it was—my oldest daughter, Jalia.

"Aye, y'all pipe down wit' the crazy talk ... I'm finna answer this call fo' one of my princesses," I informed them.

"A'ight," they replied in unison as I answered the call.

"Hey, Daddy," my sweet voiced angel stated the moment I said hello.

"What's up, baby girl?"

"Welcoming the first day out of school. Momma wanted me to ask you are you getting me for the summer?"

"Yes but it won't be fo' the whole summer. We have a lot of work to be done from now 'til the middle of next month."

"Okay," she replied before her mother got on the phone doing all that unnecessary shit talking.

As I shook my head, I replied, "Woman, if you don't shut the fuck up I swear I'mma make yo' hoe ass get a job. Like I told Jalia, from now 'til the middle of next month is goin' to be hectic at the shop. How in the hell am I goin' to spend time wit' her if I ain't home? Don't act stupid, broad. I'll give her an exact date when I will come get her. It most definitely will be next month."

"I knew I should've had a child with another nigga. You can't spend time with her but you make it your business to get your boys," she shot into the phone, causing me to become extremely angry.

"Now, you know that shit ain't true. I don't play those types of games. When I get one, I get all. I see now you are lookin' fo' a fight from me. You won't get it. Mane, I got shits to do. I'mma holla at cha," I told her nastily before I ended the call.

"We sure as hell knew how to pick the wrong types of bitches to get pregnant, huh?" VJ inquired loudly.

"Yep," we replied in unison as we began working on the assigned old school cars.

"Mine trying to soak me fo' everything I got," Dame stated before inhaling the blunt he had in his lips.

"Same here," we agreed.

As usual, the talk of our nothing ass baby mommas was the cue for us to finish our jobs of bringing our customers' visions to life.

"A little motivation fo' you niggas to hurry the fuck up," Gwap stated loudly before continuing, "Today is motherfuckin' payday niggas. Time to motherfuckin' eat an' play!"

"And motherfuckin' eat an' play we gon' do!" we shouted as we pumped our fists in the air.

***

"I ain't here fa no conversation. I ain't really tryin' to talk," the sweetest voice sang as I impatiently waited at the counter for the Arab man to hurry his slow ass up.

Motherfucking dude had a line longer than a hoe's dick record. I hated coming to the Kwik Shop gas station on Troy Highway. Every time, I would be in the motherfucking store more than ten minutes. It was the best store to run a skit. If you got food stamps, you could buy anything you wanted—gas, condoms, lip chap, tobacco and alcohol products.

"Got damn, he takin' fo'ever." Folks in the store stated in an aggravated tone.

"It's some bad ass bitches in this damn sto'," a random nigga to the right of me said as I glanced around me.

"I ain't here fa no conversation. I ain't really tryin' to talk," that same voiced individual sang causing me to turn towards the sound of her voice.

Damn it now. Lil' momma sexy as hell wit' those nerdy glasses sittin' on the bridge of her petite nose. She rockin' the shit out of that low haircut wit' that teal color strapped tight in her small head, I thought as I placed my eyes on a bad, bossy type of bitch.

Lil' momma, cinnamon brown ass, wore the hell out of an all-white workout attire. It wasn't the cotton kind but the nylon material or some shit like that. She stood about five foot six, probably about a good one hundred and fifty something pounds, nice-sized titties, light acne on her chest and face. Her ass and thighs had just the right amount of thickness and jingle.

"Shid, I don't want no conversation either. So, what's up," some nigga told the sweet voiced baddy, causing other niggas to agree with him, followed by giving her compliments.

"First off my nigga, clean them dirty ass shoes. Secondly, get that white shit from around the corners of your mouth, followed by brushing those dingy looking ass teeth. Don't come to me in that manner. I wouldn't dare waste my time dropping my panties for you," she uttered in an annoyed tone.

The way lil' momma went off on that nigga had him looking shamed faced while others in the store either laughed or joked on the nigga. I couldn't lie as if I wasn't one of the niggas that chuckled at her statement about the nigga. Oh boy righteously played his damn self.

"Bitch--," the dissed guy growled before he stopped speaking.

The sound of a gun being cocked was the reason he shut the fuck up. Quickly, I turned around and saw that the dissed, raggedy looking nigga was inches away from lil' momma.

"I got bond money fuck boy. Take another step and I will blow your fucking brains out," she spoke calmly.

In her right hand, lil' momma confidently held onto a gorgeous customized gold and teal .380.

Oh shit an' she sportin' them gold teeth in her mouth, I thought as my dick started to come to life at the sexy, classy with a splash of hood, boss woman.

As dusty dude backed away with his hands in the air, he apologized to lil' momma.

She nodded her head, followed by saying, "Yeah."

"Damn, Polo, what in the fuck is taking you so long up in this damn store," Joana stated with an attitude, the moment she crossed the threshold of the store's door.

"It ain't me, guh. It's this Arab man," I hissed as I tugged on my goatee.

I'm glad when this bitch get her fuckin' car fixed. I was supposed to have only Uber'd her som' dick.

"Fuck this shit. Let's just go to another store then," she announced loudly.

"Mane, go get in the fuckin' car," I snarled as I looked at her with a 'don't fuck wit' me' facial expression.

Smacking her mouth, the broad did what I said. Not in the mood for Joana's ass, I knew it was time to drop her ass off at home and highly reconsider about giving her ass another ounce of my time today. The past six months, Joana had been sweating the shit out of a nigga after we had fucked. She wanted to cuddle and act like we were in a relationship. She was cool peeps and all, but she started getting out of hand with her actions in public. I couldn't deal with a clingy, possessive broad. That shit would get a bitch out my life real quick.

Four minutes later, I strolled out of the door along with lil' momma that dissed the dusty dude. I damn near lost my mind the moment I got a whiff of her scent. Her perfume was intoxicating as hell. I didn't try to linger my eyes on her too long, but shit I couldn't help it. She had a nigga mesmerized by her appearance and her demeanor. That shit righteously had me fucked up in the head. I wasn't with the chicks that were damn near identical to me.

"What in the fuck is you looking at, Polo?" Joana yelled.

I didn't know which pissed me off the most: the fact that Joana was showing her ass or that I had to tear my eyes from lil' momma. Either way, a nigga was pissed the fuck off. Thus, I growled as I didn't say a fucking word to Joana as I ambled towards my black Tahoe.

"Oh, so your ass is deaf huh?" Joana inquired with a crazy facial expression.

Jonesin' For A Boss Chick: A Montgomery Love Story

"Guh, get the fuck in the truck an' shut up! Damn. Always got yo' lips poppin' an' shit," I nastily uttered before I opened the driver's door on my whip.

As I placed my right foot inside of my freshly cleaned SUV, I heard speakers knocking loud as fuck. I had to see who was making that noise. Low and behold, it was coming from lil' momma's way. As I scoped out the potential cars that had massive beat, none of them fit the profile other than a beauty of well-known car in most hoods of the south.

Nawl, I know she ain't got no whip or beatin' like dat. It gotta be her ole man shit, I thought as I lil' momma's head bobbing to USDA's song "Ride Tonight" as she closed the door on a teal colored 1976 Chevy Caprice sitting on gold 32-inch rims with some expensive ass rubberband tires.

Placing the rest of my body in my truck, I found myself bobbing my head with the beat of the song; that particular song was one of my late night trapping songs when the crew and I were up late nights serving dope to the fiends. As I reversed my truck, Joana's ass was glaring in my face. There was no reason for me to ask Joana why she was looking at me because she wasn't going to hear me. Yep, that's how loud the speakers were coming from the car lil' momma was riding in.

For the next ten minutes, I couldn't hear shit on my radio for lil' momma beating the block down while riding on the left side of my truck. When I say that I was super intrigued with her ass, a nigga was. I had to ask my niggas who the broad was that rode around in a bad ass Caprice. If anyone knew who she was, my crew would. I had to know who that baldheaded, sexy ass broad was that matched me to the T. Why? So that I could stay the fuck from around her!

CHAPTER TWO
Marcella 'Cella' Dorsey

I was used to niggas coming on to me. I was used to them getting mad when I curved their asses; however, I wasn't used to them trying to step in my space after I dissed their asses. I had to pull out my little pocket rocket to let a nigga and some of those ratchet bitches know that I was not the one to play with. The best thing they could do was move the fuck around.

That's why I hated coming to that hood ass store; however, it was the closest to my tattoo shop. On the contrary, I wouldn't have gotten the chance to see a fine ass, dark-skinned nigga that stood at least six foot five, buff than a motherfucker with more tattoos than me. Bushy, black eyebrows and six gold teeth at the bottom and a gold tooth on the left and right laterals—the teeth beside his big teeth—had me super logged into him until some loud mouth broad broke my attention away from him.

"Hey, Cella. Your one o'clock client is here," my part-time receptionist and one of my six besties, Shanice Bryant, stated coolly as she walked into my work station.

"Okay, send him back," I replied as I gobbled the rest of my sub sandwich.

"Alright, boo," she voiced before exiting the office.

I had to hurry up and finish the rest of my meal before I began tattooing on one of my favorite and loyal customers, VJ Willis. That foolish nigga had been rocking with me since I first started doing tatts in my parents' spare room.

"Cella!" VJ's deep baritone voice spat as he skipped in my work station with a smile on his face.

Laughing, I stood followed by asking, "What's up, guy?"

Embracing in a friendly hug, he replied, "Shit, coolin'. Ready to show off my latest tatt from the most creative an' talented woman in the state."

Curtsying like I always do when he gave me praises, I responded sweetly, "Why, thank you, sir."

While we chatted, VJ took off his shirt as I got my working area together for the hour tattoo on his right arm. Throughout the process, we talked about any and everything. There wasn't a topic that wasn't safe from us, including the topic of how he should let the broad he fucking around with go so that he could hook up with another of my besties, Crystal Rhyme.

"Boy, now, you know I ain't finna get into that with you and Crystal. I don't want to hear all that whining when shit don't go your way," I chuckled as I colored in the last section of his tattoo.

"Mane, look put a nigga on or som'," he spoke seriously.

VJ's ass been at my girl heavy since he placed his eyes on her, two years ago. Of course, she curved him then and still was.

"I'm not getting into that VJ," I told him as I looked into his light brown eyes.

"Ugh! You gotta give in an' help a nigga out. I ain't gon' do her wrong. A nigga just wanna take her thick, chocolate ass out an' have a good time ... dat's all," he stated with pleading eyes.

Shaking my head at his antics, I said, "All I'm going to say is that we will be at The Shack on Atlanta Highway tonight around ten or elevenish."

Pumping his fists in the air while yelling yes, VJ stood and checked out his tattoo in the full-length body mirror I had several inches away from the door.

"Mane, Cella, this tatt is fiyah," he praised as he ogled every inch of his sleeve.

"Thanks lovebug," I stated with a huge smile on my face.

Placing his shirt on, VJ stuck his left hand in his front pocket and pulled out a wad of cash. Peeling off a crisp one-hundred dollar bill, VJ said, "As always, your tip, woman."

"Thank you," I stated appreciatively while taking the money and sticking it inside of my sports bra.

Nodding his head like he always did, VJ asked, "Cella, why are you still single, mane? I know niggas hollin' at you an' shit. You far from ugly. You's a boss woman fo' sho'. So, what's the deal? Do I need to hook you up wit' one of my folks?"

"I highly believe I'm not relationship material. Men are intimidated by a woman that has her own. Um, no thanks to the hooking up part, VJ. I'm not interested in a relationship right now. I'm cooling on the men tip at the moment. Just living my dream of having my artwork shown on y'all's body, building an empire for my daughter and self, and enjoying getting to know myself."

"Understandable. Do you see niggas that make you turn yo' head?"

Thoughts of that nigga at the gas station earlier popped in my head as I lightly chuckled before saying, "Fuck yeah."

"When you ready to get in the datin' scene, I'll help you out since you dropped the dime on where y'all gonna be tonight."

"A'ight."

"I'm serious."

"Me too, VJ," I replied looking at his athletic body, six foot two, dark brown frame.

Nodding his head with a raised eyebrow, he said, "I see you brought Tealy out today. So, you need to be extra careful. You know I don't mind peelin' a nigga cap back."

Tealy was my teal and gold 1976 Chevy Caprice I had since I was twenty years old.

"You already know I keep my little pocket rocket on me, and I got them rocket launchers with me," I stated, referencing to my hand gun and assault rifles.

"A'ight. Call me if a nigga try to move som' that you can't handle."

"You gotta say that every time I bring out Tealy?" I laughed.

"Yep."

Nodding my head, I told him okay — like I usually do.

Before he exited my work station, VJ said, "Aye, Cella, are you extremely busy next weekend?"

"No. What's up?"

"A nigga need yo' help bad at the shop."

"What kind of car?" I asked excitedly with a huge grin on my face.

VJ and some of his cousins owned a customized automotive shop. They did everything from working under the hood, to painting cars, to rebuilding motors and transmissions.

Laughing, he responded, "You are a true grease monkey an' it's a '64 Chevelle."

My eyes were huge as the moon on a full night. If he needed my expertise, I was willing to give it him.

"Fuck yeah, I'm free. I don't care what you need help with. I'm in on that gig."

"That's why I fucks wit' yo' ass the long way. You already know breakfast an' lunch is on me, an' I'll put some money in yo' pockets fo' helpin' us out."

"Cool."

Shortly after we said our goodbyes, VJ was on his way out of my establishment. I was excited as hell that he asked me to help him work on a 1964 Chevy Chevelle. My grandfather and dad were the reasons why I loved fixing and rebuilding big parts to cars and trucks. To this day, I thank them highly for placing me in that setting because it had made me lots of money; damn near more money than tattooing.

Shanice informed me that my next client was present. I quickly cleaned my area, followed by setting up the things I would need. While doing so, my baby daddy sauntered his sorry ass across the threshold of the door.

"Cella," he called out.

"Yeah, LaJuan," I stated calmly.

"Um, I'm not going to be able to help you out with Xyla's birthday party."

Sighing heavy as I rolled my eyes, I shot back, "Good damn thing *her* momma busts her ass for her, huh? If it's not one thing with you, it's another. First, it was that you couldn't spend time with her this summer because you picked up extra hours at work. Then, it went to you seeking another job because the other one cut your hours. I swear I'm about to show you who you are really fucking with, LaJuan."

Every weekend since Xyla's been on this earth, LaJuan was on some fuck shit. Last weekend, it was something about his saggy, soggy titty ass mama. The weekend before that it was something about a damn ingrown toenail. It was always something with his ugly, fine ass. That nigga of a daddy had me wanting to become the worst bitch that he would ever encounter. Eight years ago, when I learned of my pregnancy, I prayed day and night that he would do right by our child even though he couldn't do right by me. Boy, was I fucking wrong!

"See, my mone--," he stated before I cut him off.

"First off all, you started the sentence wrong ... talking about *see*. I tell you what, just do you man. I'm so damn glad that I don't depend on you for shit. You gonna regret how you are doing my baby. You gonna wish that you done right by her nigga. Have a good day, LaJuan," I voiced in a semi-hostile timbre.

"Cella, look--."

"Get out of my shop before I lose my damn mind!" I voiced loudly and sternly before I pointed at the white handbag I had my pocket rocket in.

With his hands in the air while nodding his head, he voiced, "I don't want no smoke with you Cella."

"Then, be gone. Your presence is for the birds, guy."

As he looked at me, I said, "Shanice, I'm ready for my next appointment, love."

That was his cue to really get the fuck out of my eyesight before I did and said some shit that was going to hurt his entire soul. I didn't know what in the hell possessed him to think that he was going to play with my baby's feelings. Nawl, I wasn't that type of female to keep letting him walk all over her as if she didn't have feelings. I would kill about that chunky, beautiful princess I gave birth to.

"Hey, honey. How are you?" my next client asked sweetly as she stepped across the threshold of the door.

"I'm good and you, love?"

"Nervous, excited, and oh did I say nervous," she stated in a shaky voice.

Chuckling, I replied, "I was the same way when I got my first tattoo. Now, look at me with both of my sleeves, half of my left thigh, and my entire right leg has a masterpiece on it."

"Wow," she voiced in an amazed tone.

As we talked lightly, getting to know each other, I couldn't get that bastard LaJuan off my mind as I contemplated about going to the courthouse and filing for full custody of our daughter. I was going to show him that I nor Xyla wasn't pressed for him to be in her life. He was going to learn to play with his baldheaded ass momma more so than playing with me. He was going to feel what I kept telling him since I gave birth to our daughter.

I'mma make that bitch hair come off his motherfucking head, I thought as I finished tatting my client.

CHAPTER THREE
Polo

Friday night

"You been at that damn shop all day and half of the evening. When are you plannin' on spendin' som' time wit' me?" Joana asked loudly into the phone.

"You know I ain't wit' spendin' all that time an' shit. You know I ain't lookin' fo' no woman, right nih. So stop pesterin' me 'bout it. You righteously gettin' on my nerves wit' that shit."

"I'm yo' ole lady when that dick in me ... I'm yo' ole lady when it ain't in me," she replied smartly.

With a crazy look upon my face, I glanced at my phone and shook my head. Joana had been bugging me ever since I dropped her ass off at home. Numerous texts and calls about us being in a relationship had me ready to get her ass out of my life for good. Once again, the bitch was doing too much. In the beginning, I did consider Joana and I getting into a relationship; however, shit took a turn one night, and I hadn't been able to look at her the same since.

Sighing heavily while spraying cologne on my black collared Ralph Lauren shirt, I said, "Aye, woman, we ain't in no relationship wit' or without my dick stuffed in ya. Nih, we just kickin' it. The way you been actin' lately, I'm highly thinkin' 'bout cuttin' yo' ass off ... fo' good. A nigga need to breathe an' you ain't allowin' me to do that."

"I'on wanna hear none of that shit you are talking about Polo." She shot back while smacking her lips.

"You know what, Joana," I said, rubbing my hands through my goatee.

"What?" she asked with an attitude.

Click.

I ended the call. I didn't have time to be dealing with the chick that started to make me sick to my stomach. Joana and I had known each other since we were in grade school. She always had a soft spot for a nigga, but I never acted on it — until a year ago. I was on that damn Gin, and next thing you know, she was sucking the shit out of a nigga dick and doing girlfriend shit.

Ring. Ring. Ring.

Looking at my phone, I shoved that motherfucker in the black holster which was attached to my black jeans. I wasn't stun' Joana's skinny, big titty ass. She wasn't going to mess up my mood of chilling with my niggas. It's been a long time since all of us hung out together without discussing the next work load.

Ding. Dong.

"I know damn well that broad ain't pull up at my spot," I voiced as I descended down my stairs as my phone rang.

Pulling it out of the holster, I saw my cousin's, Gwap, name displaying on the screen. With a smooth swipe of my left thumb, I said, "Yo'."

"Brang yo' slow dressin' ass out tha doe mane," his deep tone spat while he inhaled what I knew was a blunt.

"I'm walkin' out nih, nigga," I responded before I ended the call.

Before I stepped out the door, I made sure to grab the pre-rolled fat blunts, mints, cigarettes, and my keys. Knowing that I been tucked my tool in the back of my jeans, I waltzed out the door as if I was the man of the hour.

"Aye, yo', Joana let yo' ass come out the crib tonight?" Dame joked after he let down the window.

"Mane, I'm a single nigga doin' single shit. Ain't no broad gon' tell me what I can an' can't do," I stated sternly with a raised eyebrow as I hopped in the front seat, greeted by a train of thick smoke.

"You gon' make dat guh do som' to yo' ass," Ponytail stated before laughing as the other fool heads chimed in with their two cents.

"Mane, my sisters will take care of her ass if she step to me the wrong way," I voiced in a matter-of-fact timbre.

My sisters didn't play the radio when it came down to broads talking to me out the side their necks. Hell, I had to get their approval before I dealt with a broad on a relationship tip. If I didn't, it would be hell to pay.

"True," they replied as the jokester of the night came in with the fuckery.

Black ass Russell Willis, aka Russ, spat, "Look at dis nigga here … motherfucka swear he finna be on the cover of XXL. You got them hoes ready to drop their pannies on site my nigga. I wanna be like you when I grow up."

"Shut the fuck up, nigga." I laughed as fired up one of the pre-rolled blunts.

Reversing from my apartment, we dapped each other up and talked shit.

Halfway out of the apartment complex, VJ said, "I know we said that we weren't going to discuss work today, but I forgot to tell y'all niggas that I got another person coming in next weekend to help out on some of our workload. She'll be helping me with the Chevelle."

"*She?*" we asked as I turned my head to look at him.

Chuckling, he replied, "Yeah, niggas, *she* an' *she* good wit' the type of shit dat we do. I'm gonna set her pockets right so I'on wanna hear y'all's mouth 'bout dat."

"Well, since you put it like that then nigga … if som' shit fall south then you gon' take the fall fo' it," I stated seriously as I wasn't too bright with his idea of bringing a broad into our shop.

Truth be told, I didn't like any outsiders working with us. We built the shop to what it was, and I wasn't with anyone coming in after we put our blood, sweat, and tears into building a name for ourselves. Dame, Big, Ponytail, Gwap, VJ, Russ, and I did what we had to do to ensure that we didn't have to work for anyone other than ourselves. Since we were youngins' our grandfather had us underneath cars, teaching us everything that we needed to know so that we could fix our own shit while getting money for fixing other folks' shit.

"So, what in the fuck are we gettin' into tonight?" Ponytail asked after he exhaled.

"Let's see what the casino hittin' fo', then we need to hit up The Shack," VJ voiced.

Nodding my head in agreeance to VJ, the others said, "Dat's a bet."

My phone vibrated long and hard. Taking it out of the holster, I saw that I had several missed calls from Joana and four text messages from her. Shaking my head, I placed my phone back in the holster. Ready for a night with nothing but pure fun, I let the seat back a little more than what it was and enjoyed the weed and my fam.

We were talking shit when all of a sudden speakers started knocking loud than a motherfucker. With a raised eyebrow, a nigga started looking around for that teal and gold Caprice. Instantly, the thought of seeing lil' momma from earlier today had my dick coming to life. As we slowly approached a red traffic light, so did a white on white, new model Range Rover with tinted windows — shaking the shit out my cousin's truck.

I didn't know the name of the song that was playing, but whatever it was it caused two light-skinned thick bitches to step out of the truck — shaking ass while their titties bounced. Of course, my niggas and I looked at the bitches doing their thing. I felt a whiff of the humid heat; thus, I knew one of them niggas rolled down the window. Turning around, I saw Ponytail and Dame hanging out the window flinging money towards the bitches. The thicker of the two scooped the money up.

When the light turned green, they hopped their thick asses in the SUV. The driver skrt'ed off as Gwap was right on the SUV's ass. Those broads had my cousins' noses wide open. They had a weakness for pretty women that could shake their asses better than a stripper. Meanwhile, I sat my ass in the front seat pissed off that it wasn't the chick whipping the hell out of the teal and gold Caprice.

Wanting to ask my peeps about the broad, it was useless because they wouldn't be able to hear me. Pulling out my cell phone, I texted VJ.

Me: Aye, man, who drive a '76 teal an' gold Caprice?

Several seconds later, he replied with: *My tattoo artist, Cella. That's who's comin' to help us out next week. Why, nigga?*

With bucked eyes, I thought, *Oh, fuck no. Nawl, she ain't bringin' her fine, bossed up ass in dat damn shop. She bad news fo' me."*

Me: No reason. But, um, you need to rethink her comin' to the shop. Serious shit. I'on know nothin' 'bout her.

VJ: Meanwhile, you askin' 'bout her an' shit. Get the fuck out of my phone wit' dat shit, Polo!!

Shaking my head at the nigga's response, I sighed heavily as I saw the Range Rover swerve from lane to lane — obviously, eager to get to their destination.

Jonesin' For A Boss Chick: A Montgomery Love Story

The loud thumping of the speakers ceased the further the SUV raced up the Boulevard. With lil' momma on my mind, I knew that I had to do something about my inquisitive mind of a woman that matched my fly to the T. How was I going to do it? I sure as hell didn't know, but I had to try something.

I can come off as an asshole to keep her ass away from me, I thought as Dame's slurred ass spoke.

"Mane, go find them bitches."

"On som'," Ponytail, Russ, and Big responded in unison.

The chatter kicked off about the thick bitches that shook their asses in the streets as if it wasn't anyone's business. While they talked, I thought about the baldheaded, glasses wearing, thick thighs, juicy booty chick that had a nigga thinking about and running from her — all at the same damn time.

Now, who can fuck in this type of weather?

CHAPTER FOUR
Cella

Tonight had been one hellava night out with my girls as we welcomed the first day of summer and kid-free celebration. Like Xyla was with her grandparents so were my besties children were with their grandparents. We had been planning this weekend ever since spring break. Shanice, Tyanna, Crystal, Sunny, Vanice, Ke'Lena, and I had been counting down the days until we were able to show our natural asses as if we were carefree teenagers again.

Who would've known that Ke'Lena and Vanice would hop their asses out of my truck and dance in the middle of the Boulevard? Sure as hell wasn't me. The killer moment that had me in tears was when Ke'Lena's crazy ass stopped dancing to pick up the money some niggas threw at them.

When she hopped in the truck, that heifer said, "Bitches, I see now I'm finna shout out them random ass niggas in my next book."

I was pissy beyond weak at her statement as Sunny said while laughing, "What the fuck? Really, Ke'Lena?"

My whip was filled with laughter thanks to one of the silliest females that was in our lives.

"Sunny, these coins finna be applied to book covers, edits, an' all dat shit." Ke'Lena shot back while laughing.

"Well, got damn it now." Crystal laughed before taking a sip of her favorite drink Arizona, the kiwi strawberry flavor.

After I fled like a bat out of hell, due to a tan colored Yukon truck closely tailing me, I knew that I had to be on my P's and Q's. I was used to shit like that happening after those heifers pulled a stunt like that. Upon seeing that I put a lot of distance between the Yukon truck and my whip, I resumed the speed limit.

"I'm so ready to shake my ass until it isn't funny," Shanice spoke as I knew without a doubt that her ass was tipsy off two wine coolers.

"Well, get ready because we'll be at our destination shortly," I told her as I looked at the time on the dashboard. It read nine forty-five.

As my ladies conversed, I was in a zone of my own. My mind alternated between two beings: Polo, that fine ass nigga from the hood store, and my ugly, fine ass baby daddy. I tried my damnest not to think about either of them and the effect they had on me. Yet, my mind did what it wanted to do. I couldn't fully enjoy my Friday night with my girls, and I didn't like that one bit.

The moment I pulled into The Shack's small, yet packed parking lot, Sunny checked my ass. "Cella, I don't know what in the fuck got your mind boggled but bitch we finna have some fun. Deal with that shit on Monday."

Of course, my chicks agreed with Sunny as I casually said, "Okay."

Placing my gearshift in park, I checked the light makeup that I had applied to my oval shaped face. Seeing that my face was on point, I opened the driver's door. The humid Earth's air did a number on my lungs as I felt like I was struggling to breathe.

"Gaht damn, it's hotter than a camel's pussy out here," Ke'Lena voiced, causing me to bust out in laughter.

"I'm sicka yo' ass already," Tyanna spoke while laughing.

As we exited my SUV, I knew that being in The Shack was going to be one hellava night with my crazy ass friends. The moment we stepped inside of the compact bar and grill establishment, it was on and popping. Shots after shots after shots we had—courtesy of a group of niggas that were in our faces. Niggas were looking and choosing while bitches had a 'stank' expression plastered across their faces.

Two and a half hours after we had been in The Shack, my eyes landed on *that* fine ass nigga dressed in all-black with two gold chains around his neck, studded earrings, a bracelet on his right wrist, and a watch on his left wrist. As he strolled behind VJ with a blunt in his mouth, his ass was looking around the establishment. With a wicked smile on my face, I glared at Crystal as she had no idea that I set a trap for her to be around VJ. Whenever she learned of what I did, she was surely going to curse me the fuck out!

"Bitchhh, do you see them stallion of niggas that just strolled through that damn door?" Ke'Lena asked excitedly.

"Yes, I did," I stated, trying not to sound aroused or elated by seeing Mr. Polo.

As I took a sip of my drink, Vanice ass rolled in front of me and drunkenly yelled in my ear, "Bitch, I saw them six foot something niggas roll up in this bitch and my pussy told my soul get ready issa fucking all night long."

With my cup to my lips, mouth filled with liquid, all that shit came out. I was laughing my ass off as VJ and his crew followed him—stopping inches away from me and my girls. Even though the music was loud as hell in the bar and grill, it didn't stop VJ from introducing his cousins to us. Each of the guys shook our hands followed by saying what's up — well, let me rephrase that better. After I shook hands with the guys that VJ introduced me too, one in particular, Polo, had an issue with touching my hand. On top of that, he gave me a dry head nod and what's up.

Taken aback, I had to laugh at the nigga. I couldn't lie as if my feelings weren't hurt because it was. The dude straight curved my ass like I did something to him. Trying to get the ill feelings I possessed to go away, I guzzled the rest of the Gin that was left in my plastic cup. Plopping the cup on the bar, I informed the bartender that I wanted another cup of Gin on the rocks — light rocks at that.

While waiting on my drink, one of my favorite local jams blasted through the speakers — LK Snoop and Sk8 song "Dance Fa Da Gwap". I knew tonight I was going to do some ass shaking; thus, I was super glad that I decided to wear a crop top, white shirt and high-rise black, tight fitted shorts, and the new white and black Jordan's. Absolutely feeling my song, the liquor, and the need to get rid of the ill feeling of getting curved by Polo, I rolled my little onion booty until I received my liquor.

Jonesin' For A Boss Chick: A Montgomery Love Story

Once it was in my hand, I sexily ambled my thick ass inches away from my ladies and the fellas. Rapping along with the song, I gave motherfuckers around me a reason to stare. It didn't take long for Ke'Lena and Vanice to be right beside me shaking ass and titties. Looking at the bar, Tyanna, Crystal, and Shanice were vibing to the beat of the song. Their asses never danced, on the dance floor that was. They were stand up or sit in the chair and move around type of chicks. No matter how lit we got those heifers never hit the dance floor like Ke'Lena, Vanice, and me.

Before I turned my head forwards good enough, I saw VJ stepping in front of Crystal. Snickering, I continued dancing along with the beat until another jam blasted. I motherfucking lost it hearing Dem Hard Headz featuring King South's song "All I Know". A bitch couldn't tell me shit as I rapped along to Burn'Em's verse. I made sure to give Mr. Polo's stuck-up ass a reason to hate that he curved me. Halfway through the song, I was shoved from the back—damn near falling on my face.

"What the fuck!" I yelped as I turned around and saw a light-skinned broad glaring at me with a severe mean-mug on her long, rounded face.

In a flash, my bitches surrounded me—saying shit that I couldn't comprehend for the music playing at a loud decibel. As the broad pointed her fingers at me, she mouthed some shit that I couldn't understand. Instantly, I was in defense mode.

Eager to know what the hoe's problem was, I stepped to the bitch. Nose to nose, I didn't give her time to say or move before I slung my damn head into hers. As she hit the ground, my sorry ass baby daddy ran over to the bitch's side. While the bold bitch was helped to her feet by LaJuan, she held her head. LaJuan shoved the skeezer behind him before acting like he wanted to hit me. Oh, why did he raise his hands at me? I surely didn't know but VJ and his crew stepped in. The fact that my daughter's father raised his hand at me caused me to become madder than a bitch finding out that she was pregnant again after seeing her doctor on her six weeks checkup.

"I just know motherfuckin' well you ain't raised yo' mothefuckin' hand at Cella, nigga," VJ spoke. The music was bumping loudly; yet, I could read his lips and so could others that were around us.

I pulled VJ backwards while saying, "Oh, I can handle this fuck ass nigga."

"Are you sure?" he asked me with his eyes on LaJuan.

As I nodded my head, I fired that sorry ass baby daddy of mine face up. The nigga was shocked at the force I brought to his face. To the point, I knew that he knew that I wasn't up for his antics. Snatching his ass by the collar of his non-name brand shirt, I politely pulled his ass out the entrance/exit door — with VJ walking behind the nigga.

"Boy, I know yo' face hurt. Lil' sexy slapped the dog shit out of yo' ass!" a deep voiced male announced into the microphone before laughing, causing everyone else to laugh.

Turning around, I shook my head at VJ followed by mouthing for him to stay inside. His didn't like what I told him; yet, he did what I told him. VJ didn't like LaJuan; he had wanted to stomp his ass out for a long time now. However, I never gave him the chance to do so.

The moment I had that ugly fine ass nigga out of the bar-grill facility, I laid his ass out.

"Did you send that bitch at me, LaJuan?" I growled as I shoved him up against the red bricked wall.

"Calm down, Cella," Tyanna and Crystal stated in unison.

"Fuck his ass up," Ke'Lena, Vanice, and Shanice chanted with their drunken asses.

"Do I look like I would send a bitch at you?" he asked, trying to break free of the hold I had on his ass.

"You know like I know that you can't get out of this hold, and if you try I will knock you the fuck out. You forgot who you are really fucking with, huh?" I stated as I kicked him in the balls.

"Ahh! Fuck, Cella!" he screamed out.

Wanting to wear his face out, I didn't. Shaking my head at the pathetic nigga, I backed away. At that moment, I knew that LaJuan was going to be a big problem if I didn't get the far away from me. I really wanted to hurt him so badly that he wouldn't be able to walk again—for the rest of his raggedy ass life.

"What in the fuck possessed you to raise your hand at me, LaJuan?" I questioned.

Shrugging his shoulders, he groaned from pain, "I don't know."

"Yes, you do. Bitch ass nigga!" Ke'Lena spoke as rolled up on LaJuan.

She was getting ready to pop that nigga in the mouth; luckily, I grabbed her hand in time enough.

"We are supposed to be having fun, and not entertaining this nigga ... remember?" I told her before I sighed heavily as another of my jams blasted from the bar and grill's speakers.

Looking at my girls, I smiled while dancing along to the beat of Doe B's song before saying, "Doe B said he got ten freaky girls taking shots and pussy popping. So, I guess I need to be in there popping pussy instead of worrying about this lame, huh?"

"You fuckin' right," they shouted in unison.

"You got saved once again by my chicks. I suggest you thank them," I told him sternly as I turned on my heels to go back inside.

I didn't make it far before the bitch that I head butted came out the door talking severe shit. Behind her were VJ and his cousins with blank looks upon their handsome faces.

"How in the fuck can you keep a man that wants to be in his child's life away from his child? Bitch, you ain't shit!"

"Go get in the fucking car, Rissa!" LaJuan stated loudly and sternly as my girls gave that bitch some choice words.

"I ain't going nowhere. You are my man. I said what you couldn't say. Damn it. She mad because she can't have you!" she loudly responded before Ke'Lena wrapped her hands around the bitch's think neck.

"Shit, Ke'Lena. Apply more pressure to the bitch's neck," Vanice laughed as Crystal, Tyanna, and Shanice agreed with Vanice.

Placing my eyes on my sperm donor, I glared at him as if he was the scum of the earth.

"So, *I'm* keeping you away from *our* daughter now," I chuckled as I clenched and unclenched my fists.

Continuing, I calmly said, "So, I'm the bad person in this picture when you are the one that keeps making promises to her and then not falling through. So, I'm the bad person because I keep giving you chance after chance to be in her life, and you refuse to do right by her. So, I'm the bad person, huh, LaJuan? You got folks rolling up on me about our child … a child that you barely do for and hardly see? So, I'm the bad person when she says that she's tired of you lying to her and not loving her like you do your other kids. I'm the bad one, huh? Well, got damn it, I guess I need to play my part, huh? Oh, I want you? Really, is that the lie that you telling these frog shaped bitches … that I want you. Bro, I got my own *everything*. Marcella Dorsey name is on the land that I own, the house that sits on it, the shop that I own, and the cars that I drive. Why would I want you when I can have any nigga that I want? What do you have that I want? Absolutely shit. You are the reason why I would never give another nigga a chance with my heart. Dude, take one of my guns and shoot yourself in the mouth. Please, please, blow your tongue off first before you seal the deal on your ending worthless life."

"Rissa, let's go," LaJuan stated softly as his eyes were low to the ground.

Ke'Lena released the bitch.

The moment Rissa walked passed me, the hoe said, "You still ain't shit."

Sinisterly laughing at the dumb broad, I said, "This pussy and head game of mine on wham. Cooking skills on damn. Business flowing like bam. Thus, I'll always be the shit, bitch!"

"Ayyyeee!" my bitches said loudly.

Not feeling The Shack anymore, I told my ladies, "I'm ready to go. Let's go grab something to eat."

"Please don't tell me that we are turning it in early," Vanice whined.

"Y'all already know what mood she's in, so let's get something to eat and see how fast we can change that mood of hers," Tyanna stated soothingly as VJ stepped in my face.

"You want me to shoot off in that nigga whip?"

Shaking my head, I lowly said, "No."

"Look at me, Cella," he said sternly in that deep voice of his.

Doing as he commanded of me, the tears welled in my eyes.

"Suck dat shit up. You bet not let na'an damn tear fall from yo' eyes. That nigga don't deserve to be in Xyla's life. She's too good fo' him anyways. Do what you gotta do, an' if a motherfucka come fo' you … yo' ass better dial my number."

Once he finished his sentence, that nigga walked off on me while firing up a blunt. Shortly afterwards, his cousins were in step behind him, heading to the parking lot.

"Bitch, the way VJ just spoke to you got my pussy percolating. I need him to talk to me in that manner. Let me go see can I get that disrespectful tone. Shat!" Crystal stated in a serious tone, causing us to laugh.

That heifer waltzed off in the direction the fellas did. She was halfway towards his car when he yelled, "Mane, get y'all asses in dat Range Rover an' follow me. Food on me an' my fam."

"You ain't gotta tell me twice!" Shanice, Ke'Lena, and Vanice yelled as they rushed to my SUV.

"What are we gonna do with those four heifers?" Tyanna asked while laughing.

"Love their foolish, semi-manners having asses," I replied as we sauntered towards my whip.

CHAPTER FIVE
Polo

Saturday, May 26th

"Yesss!" Joana cooed as I roughly shoved my dick in and out of her wet pussy.

With a fistful of her weave, I tried my best to get images of Cella out of my mind. The more I dug into Joana's deep pussy the more I fantasized that I was shoving all eleven inches of my dick inside of the cinnamon brown goddess.

"Fuck me!" Joana whined repeatedly as I pounded her pussy out.

Ding. Dong.

My doorbell dinged at the same time my cell phone rang. While fast, deep stroking Joana, I peeped on the nightstand table to see who was calling me. It was VJ.

Snatching up the phone, I said, "Yo'."

"Yes, Polo ... fuck me just like--," Joana moaned before I shoved her face in the pillow while dogging her pussy out—well more so than what it had already been dogged out.

"Well, got damn it now," VJ laughed in the phone.

"I'm almost done, nigga. What you want?"

"Shid, Crystal an' the ladies invited us to Lake Martin. Cella's lake house. We came to see if you wanted in," he asked.

As bad as I wanted to say yes, I told him no.

"Why not?"

"I got better shit to do than sit 'round at a lake house."

"Oh, like matchin' boxin' a pussy out dat barely got any walls?"

"Precisely," I laughed.

"Nigga, you see Cella as a threat to you ... don't it?"

Yep, I thought as I said, "Nigga, I'm not 'bout to have a full conversation wit' yo' motherfuckin' ass while I'm gettin' my protected dick wet."

I didn't give him time to respond before I ended the call. Thirteen pumps later, my balls ejected the nut into the Magnum condom and I was standing over the toilet to ensure that motherfucker went down the small hole.

Rubbing my back, Joana asked, "Will I get a round two?"

"Nope, you can put yo' clothes back on an' go on home," I told her with no emotions.

"What is up with your attitude, Polo?" she questioned.

"Do what I say an' we won't have any problems," I replied the moment I placed my eyes on her long, light-skinned, pretty face.

Shaking her head, she slowly waltzed down my stairs. Naked, I walked behind her ass. I wasn't about to jump in the shower thinking she was gone and the bitch was sitting on my sofa. Quickly retrieving her clothes, Joana put them on while she sniffled. I hoped she didn't think her tears were going to move me because they didn't.

Five minutes later, I locked my door, followed by opening the refrigerator. Seeing that I had a Corona in the door, I snatched that motherfucker up and opened it. As I waltzed up the stairs, I guzzled the beer all the while thinking about the one woman that I didn't want, yet wanted.

"Why in the fuck are you invadin' a nigga's mind like that woman? I ain't yo' lick. I don't need you in my life fuckin' up shit. I like the bachelor life that I have. What is it gon' take fo' me to not be so intrigued by you?"

***

"Woe, you should've brought yo' ass up here," Ponytail stated as I overheard music and happiness in the background.

"Nawl, I had some shit to sort out," I halfway lied.

"Like what?"

"Now, that's none of yo' business nigga," I said as my line beeped.

Looking at my phone, I saw Jalia's name displaying across the screen.

"Aye, Ponytail, let me hit you back, Jalia on the other line."

"A'ight. Tell her I said hey."

"Will do," I replied, quickly before clicking over to chat with daughter.

"What's up, baby girl?" I stated casually to my thirteen-year-old.

"Nothing. Just wanted to talk to you before I go to bed," her sweet voice spoke, bringing a smile to my face.

For forty-five minutes, Jalia and I talked. She was so much like me until it wasn't funny. Whenever she start dating, she was going to be hell just like me. Super smart she was with a slick mouth piece, she had that. She got that shit from her mother. Someone I keep at a distance. Jalia's mother and I can't be in the same room more than five minutes before a heated argument come about. She was still bitter about me cheating on her with my second baby mama.

After the call ended with my first-born, I called my second child, Alana. That eleven-year old character had me cracking up from the time she answered the phone until we ended the call. She was goofy as hell and smart. She didn't have a smart mouth like Jalia, but she had a mean ass way of putting you in your place. Alana got that from my mother. That woman didn't curse at all but by the time she's done telling you off, you'll feel as if she did use every curse word in the book. Alana's mother and I weren't getting along too well, now. I had to stop knocking her ass off every now and again; us having sex created problems I wasn't up for. She wanted us to be in a relationship, and I wasn't hearing that shit. So to kill the noise of us being together again, I had to deaden the shit.

Then, I called my boys. Madison Junior and Jonah were nine year old twins, spitting image of me with their mother's sneaky ass eyes. We talked about guy shit: football, girls that called themselves liking them, and the new nigga their mother was using. My boys liked the dude and he was respectful towards them so I didn't have anything to worry about. Close towards the end of the call, I told them that I needed them to call their sisters and discuss where they wanted to go for their summer vacation. As we said our goodbyes, their ugly ass mother got on the phone talking some shit I didn't want to hear. Thus, I ended the call on the raggedy ass bitch.

Ring. Ring. Ring.

Looking at my phone, I saw my mother's name on the screen. Outstretching on the sofa, I answered the phone.

"Hello, Son. How are you?"

"I'm good. How 'bout you?"

"Good. Um, I want to hear your side of the story ... concerning you and Joana."

I just know damn well that crazy ass broad didn't call my momma wit' that fuck shit, I thought as I said, "What you talkin' 'bout , Momma?"

"You know good and well what I'm talking about Madison Marcell Willis. Are you mistreating her? Are you playing games with that woman?"

Sighing heavily, I didn't say a word as she repeated her statement again, a little louder. I couldn't lie to my momma or half-ass tell her the truth. Therefore, I told her the truth.

"Momma, I'm not feelin' Joana like that. She cool an' all, but I don't see me settlin' down wit' her. Honestly, I don't see myself settlin' down wit' anybody's daughter no mo'. I'm don' wit' that love thing. The way things played out between Madison Junior an' Jonah's mammie, I ain't willin' to give anotha woman my time, patience, loyalty, an' dedication. I told Joana from the jump I didn't want a relationship."

"You never thought about it or mentioned it to her?"

"I sort of played 'round wit' the idea but deep down I knew that's not what I wanted."

"Son, you too dang old to be playing the field. That's something you do when you are young. You are about to be thirty six this year. You need to find the one that makes your heart flutter at the thought of her. You need to stop being afraid to love someone that's not your family. Honey, you need to let that situation that occurred between you and Janah go. She did what she did. You need to forgive her so you can live a happy life with someone that can bring you the best joyful life."

As my mother talked, I thought about the way Janah did a nigga. She was the reason I went to prison for ten years. The bitch said she was going to ride for me and wait until I got released from prison. Tuh, that bitch left me mentally fucked up. Like most dope boy loving bitches do, Janah hopped on another nigga's dick and forgot about the shit that she had told me. Before she fled the state with our two-year old sons to be with the nigga, that hoe stole my hidden dope and money. It wasn't long before Janah got what she deserved. The nigga she left the state for started tearing her fucking head off every damn time he felt like it.

I swore that I would never forgive Janah for what she did to me and how she tried to brainwash my boys into thinking that I didn't want or loved them, and I haven't to this day.

"Son," my mother's sweet voice called out, bringing me into reality.

"Ma'am."

"You aren't getting any older, Son. Let someone in so that you could be a true blessing to them as they are to you. Son, you have a beautiful heart. Let someone see it other than your family. If you don't, you are going to let life pass you by because you are afraid of getting hurt again. Madison, you deserve happiness and love too. If you don't see it with Joana, seek it elsewhere. Don't do anyone the way you were done. Heart break is heart break at the end of the day. Don't be ugly to someone else just because it was done to you."

"K, Momma," I stated.

"Now, we got that out of the way. In three weeks, there will be the pastor's anniversary at the church and I expect your tail to be there. Understood?"

"Yes, ma'am," I replied as I quickly envisioned my head smoking the moment I step through the church doors. Oh, the perks of having your father as a pastor and your mother as the first lady—damn sure ain't priceless.

"Love you, Momma."

"Love you, more, Son. Think about what I told you."

"I will."

"Goodnight."

"Goodnight, Momma."

There was no need in heavily thinking about what my mother said to me. I know she was right, but I refused to be taken down that road again. I wasn't up for my heart to be shattered into pieces. That shit was for the birds, and I sure as hell wasn't one.

CHAPTER SIX
Cella

Saturday, June 2nd

It had been a long week. My thought process was all over the place as I contemplated petitioning for full custody of Xyla. I didn't see the need in asking for child support. Hell, I made damn good money. I didn't see the need in having LaJuan with parental rights if he wasn't going to do right. Still, it was a hard decision to make. Thus, it kept entering my mind. She was too young for me to tell her the truth; hell, even I didn't know the truth — well, fully. I just knew what I saw from his actions and the things that he said. He acted like he didn't want to be in her life.

"Aye, Cella, you ready to get the day started?" VJ asked the moment he walked from the back of the garage.

"And you know that I am," I stated happily as I looked at our project for the day.

"Good. Cause I plan on havin' this sucker ready fo' my customer by three-thirty."

"I figured that since the damn sun isn't up yet," I voiced quickly before continuing, "So, what exactly do you need my help with?"

With a wicked smile on his face, VJ replied, "The speaker knockers."

In a high-pitched tone I yelled, "I know motherfucking well you didn't have me up at this damn shop at three in the morning for some fucking speakers and amps!"

Laughing as he strolled towards the car, he said, "Yep."

"I'm finna go get my ugly ass in the bed. Call me when you are done with your job. Then, I will do my job."

"No ma'am. He wants the amps rebuilt … better."

More excited than a bitch telling the top notch dope boy that she was pregnant, I was! It was something about rebuilding anything that made my loins jump for joy. I was overly happy to begin looking at what the customer had.

"I thought that would change yo' damn tune." VJ laughed as the back door of the garage opened, followed by the fellas walking in — greeting us. Just like a week ago, Polo spoke to me dryly. I reciprocated the same attitude towards him.

The early morning hours flew by as we listened to music, talked, and joked—well, minus Polo. The only time he talked to me was when he asked for me to rebuild an amp that he fucked up when installing it. Quickly, I helped his fine ass out and went on about my business.

At noon, I said, "So, am I done?"

"No, please don't leave, Cella. We love seein' Polo sweatin' an' shit," Ponytail laughed, causing the others to laugh—minus Polo and me.

"Ain't nobody sweatin', nigga. Fuck ya mean?" Polo growled as he looked at Ponytail.

"You's a whole damn lie. You thank a nigga ain't seen you peepin' out Cella. Dude, you ain't never fucked up an amp … ever, but all of a sudden you installin' them bitches in wrong an' shit. Blowin' the fuses on 'em an' shit," Russ spat while laughing.

"Whatever, nigga," Polo stated blankly as the guys began to joke on him for having a soft spot for me.

"Cella, ain't my type. Y'all know my type an' it sure as hell ain't her. She cool an' all but nawl. Shawty, ain't light enough fo' me."

I had to roll my eyes at dude, followed by cutting my time and their conversation short before I cursed Polo's ass out.

"I will see y'all later. VJ, just bring the money to the shop Monday."

"Um, where are you goin'?" VJ asked as if he was my damn daddy.

"Gotta help the ladies set up a surprise party at the lake house for my little lady."

"Aww," those negros, minus Polo, stated in unison.

"Are we invited?" Ponytail asked.

"Sure."

"Will it turn into a grown folks party afterwards?" Gwap questioned.

"And you motherfucking know it is," I stated before laughing.

"That's what the fuck I'm talkin' 'bout!" Big's super deep voice boomed from underneath the hood of a Monte Carlo SS.

"The grown folks party will kick off around nine after everyone leave," I told them as I strolled towards the door that connected the garage and customer service area.

"A'ight. We will be there before the kids' party kick off. I say around three-thirty or so. Call me if you need me to pick up anythin'," VJ stated as I grabbed ahold of the gold door knob.

Jonesin' For A Boss Chick: A Montgomery Love Story

"Yes sir, boss."

***

It took me forever to stop thinking about what Polo had to say about me not being his type. I hated that I didn't cut throat his ass like I did other niggas that said something slick out of their mouths about me. It ate me up that I didn't handle that nigga like he tried to handle me.

The only thing that eased my mind from feeling like I let Polo play me was my girls meeting me at the lake house to decorate the place for my big girl turning eight years old. Of course, the ass shakers put on music to help ease the tension that they saw on my face and body. After we decorated the house, each of us had a task that we had to complete.

Tyanna did the candy table for the children area, followed by setting up a table for the grown folks party. Vanice set up the seating area for the grown folks party in the front room. Shanice took care of the goody bags for the Xyla's party; there were only going to be eight family member kids in attendance since my chicks children were out of town. Sunny's ass was mixing up a concoction that was surely going to have folks passed the fuck out all over my damn lake house. Ke'Lena was doing her thing with the weed edibles — of course, for the grown folks party.

Crystal and I began preparing the food for both parties, which we were on the last food item.

"So, have you decided on what you are going to do concerning the full custody thing?" Crystal asked me while we prepared the homemade hamburger patties.

"No."

"Have he tried calling you?"

"No," I replied as I placed the nice sized raw patted meat on a silver tray.

"Have you talked to your parents about this?"

"Yes. They think it's best to leave it alone all together," I sighed as I heard the loud crew, aka The Willis crew, coming through the side door.

"Ohh, is that my boo VJ," Crystal stated as she began to glow.

Feeling as if I was out of the loop with things, I said, "Um, ma'am. Did something happen between the two of y'all after we left Denny's a week ago?"

"Yes, lawd. Yes," she voiced with a huge grin on her face.

The fellas, minus Polo, strolled into the house smelling like three pounds of weed as they held tightly onto multiple bags.

"Where is the birthday girl?" Ponytail asked.

"She, her guests, and their parents are at the lake with my parents and brother," I stated as I noticed Crystal and VJ kissing, deeply.

"Well, I be hot damn," Ke'Lena spat as she strolled into the kitchen, causing us to laugh.

"Yo' ass would be gettin' kissed like dat but yo' ass don't know how to mind yo' manners," Dame stated sternly as he placed his eyes on my girl.

"Um, what the fuck is mindin' manners when you drop dick like it's an atomic bomb?" she asked with her head cocked to the right.

"Dammnnnn!" we stated in unison.

Laughing, I said, "Wait a minute ... what else have I missed within this past week? First of all, how in the ... nevermind, y'all better get to talking."

As those fuckers gave me the rundown on what really been going on, I was one surprised bitch! Not any of my bitches told me what they had been up to or what had been up in them should I say. Shanice and Russ teamed up. Tyanna and Ponytail hooked up. Vanice and Big smashed. Last but not least, that damn Sunny and Gwap hooked up.

"Wait a fuckin' minute!" my ladies and I, minus Sunny, yelled as we looked at her.

"Um, what are you guys talking about?" she asked in that proper voice she used when she withheld information that came to light.

"Ooouu, bih, you know damn well yo' ass gotta spill all them damn beans, cornbread, collard greens, and yams!" Ke'Lena yelled.

"Big facts," I spoke loudly.

"I plead the fifth on anything, guys," she stated as she ambled towards Gwap and placed a juicy kiss on his lips.

At that sight, I damn near passed out from excitement.

"Guh, how it feel gettin' dicked down after how long now?" Vanice questioned while laughing.

"You see, Vanice, I swear that's why I do not like yo' yella ass," Sunny voiced in a joking manner before Gwap popped that little toot toot.

"No, damn wonder she lookin' all girlie an' shit lately," Tyanna stated as Ponytail strolled behind her.

"Now, we gotta get Polo on deck with you, Cella, and then we will be complete," Russ voiced.

Silence overcame us I knew I made the ugliest face. I was on the verge of saying something when I heard the children approaching.

"Let's get this party underway!" I shouted as I was ready to drink and have fun with people that were willing to have fun with me.

For the next four and half hours, the adults had fun with the kids. Not one time did Xyla ask me about her father, and not one time did I mention or think of his ass. The bastard didn't even call or text her happy birthday. That fact alone was the reason why I was going fall through with seeking full custody.

"Thank you for having me a fun party, Mommy," my sweet, chunky faced daughter stated before yawning while she gave me a hug.

"You are very welcome, lovebug," I lovingly replied as I placed eight kisses on each side of her cheeks.

"Oh, and thank y'all for my gifts," she happily announced to everyone.

"You are welcome," everyone replied in unison.

"Um, Mommy, who's Uncle Polo?"

With a raised eyebrow, I questioned, "Who?"

"Well, well, well," Ke'Lena and Big voiced in unison before The Willis crew and my girls burst out laughing.

"Uncle Polo," she stated as if I supposed to know who in the hell she was talking about.

"Sweetie, you don't have an Uncle by the name of--," I stated as I looked at VJ.

He shook his head no. Why? I had no damn idea and I sure as hell wasn't going to ask.

"Xyla, why do you want to know who he is?" I questioned as I was trying to get a better understanding of things.

"I wanted to thank him personally for my gifts."

"Um, what gifts honey?" I questioned oddly.

Clearing his throat, Dame said, "'Bout an hour after you left, Polo an' I hit up som' stores to find baby girl somethin' fo' her birthday. Butt brain didn't know what to get her so he got her a pair of J's and had them customized, eight outfits, and eight toys. Oh, and he stuffed three hundred dollars in her birthday card that he signed *Uncle Polo*."

"Hmph," I voiced sarcastically as I thought, *Wow, he isn't that much of an asshole after all huh?*

"Well, I will be sure to tell him that you said--," I stated before Gwap cut me off.

"Cella, if you don't mind, she can tell him thank you now. He on my line."

"Sure," I replied as I nodded my head.

Oh, how cute she was on the phone talking to the one man that was a complete asshole to me. Xyla brought me Gwap's cellphone, followed by saying, "He wants to talk to you."

"'Bout time," Russ said before drinking on the hunch punch Sunny made.

"Hello," I stated casually.

"Aye, Cella, I'm sorry 'bout today. I was in a bad mood. You didn't deserve fo' me to do you like that," his sexy ass stated sincerely.

"You good. Thanks for my daughter's gifts," I quickly shot back before handing Xyla the phone to take back to Gwap.

"Well, dang that was short," Ponytail spoke while looking at me.

It needed to be. He ain't my cup of tea anymore with his fine, sweet-nasty attitude having ass, I thought as my daughter's guests, their parents, my brother, and parents said their goodbyes, followed by giving my ladies and I hugs and a kiss on the cheeks. I made sure to tell Xyla to put her gift bags in her room before leaving the lake house.

"What I'm trying to understand is why your trifling ass sister didn't come?" Vanice asked.

"Because it was no money to be giving to her greedy ass." I shot back.

"But Xyla's her niece," she continued.

"Yep. Anyways, my baby ain't wanting for shit. It's a good thing the broad didn't show up anyways. She wasn't going to do anything but piss me off."

Not the one to dwell on my nothing ass baby sister Traneice, I held up a cup filled with hunch punch and yelled, "Oooou, motherfuckas let's get got damn wasteddddd!"

"'Bout motherfuckin' time!" they yelled as the explicit rap music blasted from the surround sound.

As we drank, danced, and had fun, a part of me wished that Polo would've came. He would've been nice to look at while I sneakily looked at him while having fun with the crew. His appearance was heavily needed for the aftermath of drinking and getting high. My ladies had already chosen their favorite room with their boos. Hell, I needed to see Polo so when the time came for me to play in my pussy his scent and face would be fresh on my mind.

Oh, asshole of a Polo. Oh, asshole of a Polo. What would I give to see your no manners having ass right about now? I thought as Ke'Lena yelled for us to take another shot of lemonade moonshine.

"Oouu, somebody finna do some fuckin' tonight!" Vanice yelled, causing us to yell out.

"And all motherfuckin' night long, bihhh!"

CHAPTER SEVEN
Polo

Sunday, June 3rd

From the time, Dame and I finished shopping for Cella's daughter, I laid my ass on the couch, flipping channels, and rejecting calls from Joana's whining and begging ass. I was beyond bored to the point I got mad at my damn self for not opting to attend the festivities at the lake house, and being nasty to Cella because I was afraid of connecting with her.

Every time I called one of them ugly ass niggas, it sounded like they were having a motherfucking ball. Each time they told me to come over I said I had better things to do. The third to the last time I called, I briefly talked to the sweetest voice child that I ever heard. Immediately, I put my shoes on as I asked for her to hand her mother the phone. The moment Cella got on the phone my dumb ass choked up and gave her a sincere yet weak ass apology for my antics, earlier. As I was in the process of getting ready to ask her was I still invited to the late house, she rushed off the phone. Luckily, Gwap gave me the address just in case I wanted to pop up. Yet, my dumb ass didn't leave until I had enough of fighting with myself.

Here it was one o'clock in the morning, and I was sitting in the drive of a beautiful lake house watching Cella cry while balled up in a lounge chair. As I smoked on a fat blunt, my mother's message seeped into the front of my mind. Seeing that I should — for once — take her advice, I exited my truck, ensuring to close the door lightly. I didn't want Cella to hear me creep up on her with a bouquet of roses that I copped, along the way, from Wal-Mart in Millbrook.

Inches away from her, I heard the slow jams playing as I noticed the freaks were nastily grinding on each other. Shaking my head, I lightly laughed at them.

"Dry those damn eyes woman. You are better than that," I told Cella sternly as I handed her the bouquet of roses.

Startled, she turned around with puffy red eyes and an 'oh shit' facial expression.

As she took the roses, I said, "That's a formal apology fo' my behavior lately an' a way of sayin' thank you fo' helpin' us out yesterday. Truth be told, without you, I don't think we would've gotten all the cars out of the shop."

"Thank you and no problem. VJ is one of my besties after all; so it was a pleasure helping him out."

"May I sit out here wit' you?"

"Sure," she replied softly as she looked at the ground.

"I'm not on the ground. I'm up here. So, look me in my face, Cella ... whenever we are talkin'. Understood?" I voiced sternly.

As she placed her eyes on me, she nodded her head, followed by laughing.

"What's funny?" I questioned while taking a seat close to her.

"You being demanding and shit ... me obeying like a little puppy." She chuckled.

"A cute lil' pug puppy at that." I joked, causing her to laugh.

"Don't be tryin' to play me, Polo," she cooed softly.

Clearing my throat, I said, "We got off on the wrong foot ... you know what ...I got off on the wrong foot wit' you. Can we start over or whatever?"

"Sure," she voiced before extending her hand.

Continuing, Cella said, "My name is Marcella Dorsey but my friends call me Cella, and you are?"

"I'm Madison Willis, but my fam call me Polo."

"Ahh, Madison," she voiced sexily and seductive.

The way she called my name had my heart and stomach fluttering. Oh, and not to mention my dick on hard.

Pushing my erection out of my mind, I asked, "Would you care to give me a tour of the lake?"

"Sure."

For the next hour or so, we got to know each other. Man, when I say that we had so much in common until it was unbelievable. She was exactly what I was scared of—my damn twin to the T. Yet, I let my mother's conversation play in my head until Cella dragged me in the house with the rowdy drunk crew.

"Motherfuckin' Polo!" their drunken ass yelled before they started screaming.

"Shots!"

We threw back damn near six cups of lemonade moonshine before we guzzled a cup of hunch punch. A nigga was feeling good as shit by the time I threw my cup away.

"Um, so how in the hell are we goin' to drive back to Da Gump wasted?" I asked with a raised eyebrow.

"We aren't. We are stayin' at the lake house tonight," Dame spoke in a slurred manner.

"Oh shit. Team no sleep, huh?" I asked them.

"Fuckin' all night mornin' long … all mornin'!" the paired couples shouted before we laughed.

One of my jams by Ball Greezy "U Tonight" blasted through the surround sound system, causing me to grab Cella's hand and dance.

"Okay, nih!" the freak some team yelled as they followed suit with Cella and me.

"I'm glad you decided to stop being an asshole and became friendly with me," she spoke in a slurred tone as she looked into my eyes.

Nodding my head, I replied, "Me too."

Out the midst of nowhere, I planted a kiss on her forehead.

Shocked at my actions, I quickly said, "I'm sorry."

With a smile on her beautiful face, Cella coolly responded, "No need to be sorry, Madison."

Without a doubt, I knew that she was feeling a nigga. How I knew? She called me by my government name plus she had that same twinkle in her eyes whenever she looked at me. She had that twinkle the first time I placed my eyes on her, that night at The Shack, and throughout our time at Denny's, and yesterday at the shop.

Song after song, drink after drink, and edible after edible, we enjoyed ourselves. One by one the couples began to disappear upstairs. They left Cella and I dancing to "You Belong To Somebody Else" by Dej Loaf and Jacqueez.

"Ah, this song," Cella stated as she massaged my shoulders as we slowly grooved to the song.

"What 'bout it?"

"Nothing," she replied as she shook her head.

Chuckling, I said, "Let me guess you are wonderin' 'bout the female that I was at the store wit'."

"Sort of."

"We aren't an item. We kicked it, but she ain't my type," I voiced seriously.

Busting out in laughter as she shook her head, Cella asked, "Then what in the hell is your type then?"

"You … honestly," I quickly replied as I gazed into her eyes.

There was nothing left to be said. I pulled Cella close to me and didn't tear my eyes away from hers as we danced along to the song until it ended.

The moment GQ's song "I Do Love You" blasted from the speakers, Cella pushed away from me as she began singing along with the singers. Going into a zone of her own, I wanted to pull her close to me; yet, I watched the beautiful woman enjoy the song. I could tell that the song was dear to her heart. Quickly, I thought about her thinking of a nigga that she had sung the song to. Instantly, I was jealous and pissed off.

That was until, her crew fled down the stairs in over-sized T-shirts, screaming the words to the song. As soon as Cella saw them, she became extremely emotional. Why? I sure as hell didn't know. In sync with their girl, the ladies sang and danced along as they embraced each other. As my fam stormed down the stairs shirtless, they had a crazy looking expression plastered across their faces.

The moment they stood by me they mouthed, "What the hell?"

As I shrugged my shoulders, we watched the ladies sway their hips as they shouted, "My baby, I love you sooo!

"I was in the middle of gettin' my dick rode from the side when Vanice hopped up off me talkin' 'bout she had to run downstairs," Big spat in an upset tone.

"Same here, minus the ridin' from the side," the others spat.

"Repeat that shit," Tyanna voiced loudly as the ladies agreed but my niggas disagreed.

Apparently, the ladies had to hear the song. The song was started over, and the still drunken women sauntered towards their partners as Cella danced towards me with her a huge smile on her face. As the ladies held out their hands, my niggas became putty and danced along with the beautiful women they had chosen.

Roughly snatching Cella in my arms, I growled in her ear, "What nigga got you dancin' wit' me while you thinkin' 'bout him?"

She didn't respond; yet, she sang sweetly into my ear, followed by glaring into my face and singing with perfection. I couldn't lie as if I didn't want her to be saying those words and meaning them. I couldn't lie as if I wasn't smiling like a shy ass school boy. I couldn't lie as if Cella didn't have my hardcore ass feeling like I was the luckiest nigga in the world. I couldn't lie as if I didn't have my tail tucked between my legs as she made every nerve in my body tingle.

Towards the end of the song, she softly replied, "The day I gave birth to Xyla, I couldn't say the speech that I had prepared for her; thus, I sang this song to her. Every time I placed my eyes on her, on her born day, I sang the hell out of GQ's song to the one person that would love me unconditionally — flaws and all. To this day, I sing this song to her and I get excited and emotional all over again. Thus, my ladies and I sang and remembered how it was for me on that day to transition from a childish girl into a full grown woman who was willing to lay her life down for the little one she brought into the world. That was the day I chose to change for the better. For Xyla, my everything."

The way she spoke about the sweet voiced angel, I knew that Cella was the one for me; yet, I didn't know how I was going to get over the thought of being played and left alone. The love she had for her daughter brought the soft side out of me. Not too many people could say that they saw a soft spot in me — especially, the women that I had dealt with in the past, including my baby mommas.

"The first time I saw you, you made me weak. You were my twin. My fuckin' Kryptonite. I wanted you ... then again I didn't want you. You had a nigga intrigued by yo' boss ass demeanor. Yo' swag. You murked my soul the moment you hopped inside of a teal an' gold Caprice. I knew that you were made fo' a nigga, but shid I couldn't take dat pressure you was applyin'. I couldn't get yo' ass out of my mind no matter what I did. I ain't gon' lie to you, Cella, a nigga righteously scared of you but you be on a nigga's mind too much not to see what you 'bout," I voiced softly while gazing into her dark brown eyes.

"I feel the same way," she voiced before biting on her bottom lip.

"So, what are we gonna do 'bout it?" I found myself asking, feeling like a lame nigga.

"I guess we take it slow. Be friends first, then see where that goes," she responded.

"I can dig that, but um ... I'm rusty in bein' solely friends wit' a female," I chuckled.

"Well, I guess I will take the lead on this one, huh?"

"Yep."

"Well, friend, the first thing is ... we don't have sex until we feel it is right. We get to know each other better. We do the texting and talking on the phone thing. Possibly hang out ... doing what we like to do, and stuff like that."

Nodding my head, I nervously said, "Okay."

Laughing, Cella said, "You like to play pool and so do I. We will start there, right now ... in the game room downstairs."

"Wait a whole motherfuckin' minute, you have a game room?" the fellas and I stated in unison, amazed.

"Well damn, where did y'all come from?" Cella laughed while looking at my cousins as she nodded her head.

"Fuck sex, let's get to this game room," Ponytail, Gwap, and Big shouted, causing us to bust out in laughter.

"Look at this baldheaded bitch here, bringing up the damn game room," Ke'Lena spat while laughing as Cella grabbed my hand, leading us towards the entertainment room.

Lord, please don't let me mess things up wit' Cella. She cool an' her vibe is wonderful. But, my past hurts got me ready to run for the border. Give me strength to let me see where things could go between the two of us, I thought as I exhaled softly.

CHAPTER EIGHT
Cella

"They ain't fucked out an' tired yet," Polo asked while shaking his head at the baby orgy party going on within every bedroom of my lake home.

Laughing, I said, "Hell no. My bitches can fuck all night and day. Sunny just now getting her groove back. So, I know she gonna give Gwap a run for his money."

Shaking his head, Polo looked at me with his dreamy eyes before asking, "Do we really gotta stay here as they freakin'?"

Chuckling, I replied, "No, we don't. Where would you like to go?"

"For starters, I gotta go home an' change clothes. Then, we can decide from there. Cool?"

"Cool," I replied with a smile on my face.

Slipping out of the bed, I was nervous hell as I knew that Polo was watching me. I wanted to turn around, but my nerves wouldn't let me. It was something about him that made me extremely nervous even with all of my clothes on.

At eight o'clock this morning, our time in the game room ended when the freaksome crew decided they needed to have a one-on-one session with their chosen ones. After those fuckers went to their sleeping quarters, Polo and I walked around the lake. Once he felt sleep approaching, he had the audacity to say that he was going to head home. Of course me being me, I wasn't going to let him go home after drinking and being up all day and night. Thus, I told him that he could sleep in the room with me. The moment that nigga passed out in my bed, all I could do was stare at his chocolate ass. Sleep finally found me, and apparently so did Polo's arms wrapped around me but not before he pulled me close to him.

"Don't take all day gettin' dressed nih." He snickered as I disappeared into my large walk-in closet.

"Oh, hush up, sir." I laughed.

Within seconds, I knew exactly what I was going to put on—a casual gray and olive green, knee-length, thick strapped dress and a pair of olive green plain Jane shoes. My choice jewelry was simple—silver hoops, two, small-sized studded earrings, silver ankle bracelet with my daughter and my names encrusted in diamonds, and a silver watch.

After I retrieved my attire and placed my jewelry on the chrome and platinum dresser, I rummaged through my panty and bra drawer. Seeing that my dress was a body-con, I decided that I wasn't going to put on any underwear. Quickly, I snatched a black laced bra and dashed towards my three differently shades of brown themed bathroom.

Thirty minutes later, I exited the bathroom looking absolutely breathtaking. The look on Polo's face was priceless as he licked his lips and eye fucked me.

Clearing my throat, I said, "Are you ready, sir?"

"Yes, because them niggas ain't lettin' up in this bitch," he voiced shaking his head as he stood, shoving his big ass feet into his shoes.

Before I could respond my mouth was shaped in a wide O as I heard sex noises and headboards sounding off.

"Cella, let's go," Polo groaned as he threw his shirt over his head.

I couldn't lie as if I wasn't getting aroused at what was going on around us. Those bitches were having mad fun, and here my wet, cob-webbed pussy was dreaming of some dick entering it.

Skipping passed Polo, I snatched my phone and wallet off the dresser and rapidly descended the stairs as I imagined Polo shoving me against the wall and giving me the business.

"Ooou, this dick too fuckin' bomb!" Ke'Lena groaned from the second bedroom.

After setting the alarm, Polo and I sighed heavily as we escaped the house of fucking.

"Finally, out of the fuck zone." He laughed.

"Tell me about it. Now, whose whip are we driving?" I inquired as I hoped he said we were taking Tealy out.

"I wanna know what that Caprice talkin' 'bout," he answered while rubbing his goatee.

"Cool." I beamed as I unlocked the doors on one of my favorite cars.

I started the engine, and Ronnie Bell's "I'll Pay the Shipping Cost" blasted through the speakers. As I jigged to the song, Polo laughed at me while bobbing his head along to the beat. Pulling away from one of my favorite places that I owned, I was excited to be spending my spare time with someone that piqued my interest.

Throughout the ride to Montgomery, I realized that Polo was just right for me. We had a lot of things in common. We were self-made bosses—the legit way. That was a plus in my eyes. Most niggas that stepped to me were dope or jack boys. I couldn't deal with those types of niggas for the simple fact that they wouldn't have my shit ran through or taken away from me. One thing I learned about those types of nigga, they didn't love nobody but themselves.

As we pulled into Polo's apartment complex, I became a bundle of nerves. He noticed it and spoke on it.

"I know damn well you ain't nervous or scared, woman?"

Trying to put my big girl draws on, I piped back, "No, I am not."

"A'ight," he said before telling me which apartment was his.

"I'll wait in the car."

With a smirk on his face, that nigga demanded, "Mane, get out this car an' come in."

Loving how demanding his sexy ass could be, I shut off the engine and stepped out of my car.

"Damn, Polo, dats you?" some guys to the left and right of us asked in an amazed tone.

"Nawl, an' no she ain't up fo' grabs ... eitha. Is that understood?" he spoke in a stern voice while looking ach of the guys in their faces.

"Most definitely," they announced as they nodded their heads.

Well, alrighty then, I thought as Polo held out his hand.

"Come on, woman," he sexily demanded.

***

Oh, what fun did Polo and I have as we acted like big ass kids. From taking a walk around Shakespeare Festival park to visiting a place that had several activities such as bumper cars, go-karts, laser tag, and a freefall tower. I just knew that I was going to lose my damn mind while being dropped from the highest point of that freefall. I didn't lose my mind; however, Polo did. He was big mad that he allowed me to talk him into freefalling. The moment we were high in the air, his mood changed. The second we began to rapidly descend that nigga had me cracking up laughing. He didn't yell or scream—that nigga began praying.

Afterwards, we visited another fun place called *Rockin' Jump*. I semi-enjoyed the trampoline/rock climbing facility; if I had chosen a different attire, then I knew I would've enjoyed the rock climbing more. I couldn't be carefree there as I was at the laser tag place. Now, the trampolines were fair game until Polo bounced me so high that when I came down he got a sneak peek of the cob-webbed kitty. That one sight caused him to say that it was time to go eat. With a smile on my face, I slowly exited the trampoline area; whereas Polo ran up out of the joint—holding his hands in front of him.

Jonesin' For A Boss Chick: A Montgomery Love Story

I giggled like a school girl at the sight of him. By the time I made it the entrance/exit doors, Polo yelled for me to stay where I was. Laughing, I did just that. I watched his handsome ass run to Tealy. Once inside of my whip, he eagerly reversed my whip followed by pulling up in front of me. As I reached for the door handle, Polo had opened the door for me. Feeling warm and bubbly, I slid my sexy self in the passenger seat and bit down on my bottom lip.

I didn't want anything ordinary to eat; thus, I told Polo that we should eat at a restaurant downtown called *Central*. He agreed. Soon as we arrived at the eatery, that nigga had me tickled. I could tell that he wasn't used to frequenting upscale restaurants such as *Central*. The look on his face as he surfed through the small dinner menu had tears streaming down my face.

"Mane, Cella, we been at this damn place for fifteen minutes, and I have no damn idea what the fuck I want to eat. Will you please pick out what you think I would like," he voiced seriously as he looked at me.

"Sure," I replied.

Shortly after I skimmed through the menu, our waitress—a thick-sized White woman with a beautiful smile stepped to our table—for the third time. Before I placed our food order in, Polo and I ordered our drinks. He wanted a Heineken, and I had to have a mixed cocktail drink called Creole Nights; my drink consisted of Captain Morgan rum, apple cider, lime, brown sugar, and ginger ale. Once our drink orders were in, I placed our food order. Throughout the entire time I talked, Polo looked at me with a quizzical look on his face. When the waitress left, his expression was still the same.

"What?" I asked with a pleasant smile on my face.

"Why did you choose this place?" he inquired while slouching in the comfortable dark brown chair.

"Because I love it, and I had hoped that you would like the atmosphere and the food ... basically I wanted to bring you into my world for a minute."

"So, you like a low-key, dimly lit, acid jazz playin' in the background type of environment, huh?"

"Yes. I'm able to relax and think. I come here when I've had a very stressful week, or I know I'm about to have a stressful week."

"Here are your drinks," the spunky waitress said as she sat our drinks on the table.

"Thank you," I happily stated before taking a sip of my concoction.

"Your appetizer will be up shortly," she said.

"Okay," I replied.

"Appetizer?" Polo inquired.

Nodding my head, I said, "Oh yeah."

"What exactly did you order fo' an appetizer? 'Cause I swear the shit you called out was main course meals."

"I ordered the local and domestic cheeses with fresh meats, dried fruit, and seasonal fruit preserves and house made breads."

"And they call that an appetizer?" he asked seriously.

"Yes."

"Shit, I ain't gon' lie a nigga was lookin' fo' some fried wings an' shit fo' an appetizer." He laughed.

"You ain't gettin' no fried wings tonight, homie," I stated while laughing.

"I guess not ... you better be glad that I'm willin' to try somethin' new 'cause of you," he spoke sincerely as he raised an eyebrow.

"Oh aren't I the lucky one."

"Possibly," he replied before licking his thick, juicy lips.

My oh my. I wonder how they feel, I thought as he struck up an interesting conversation that caused us to let loose as we had been all day — enjoying each other's company all the while being carefree and respectable.

Fifteen minutes later, our food was presented to us in such a beautiful way that I had to take pictures of our meal. My Atlantic Salmon dish had my mouth watering as I glared at the meat, smoked fingerling potatoes, corn pudding, and bacon and onion vinaigrette.

With a raised eyebrow, Polo looked at me with a frown on his before saying, "Nih, what kind of shit is this, Cella? What is up wit' these small ass tomatoes? What is this brown squiggly thang? Mane, what in the hell did you order me? We ain't gon' talk 'bout the amount of food that is on this nicely decorated plate. Cella, I'm a big nigga. This is not what I had in mind. On life, this is not what I had in mind."

Slapping my forehead as I chuckled at him, I said, "I ordered you a twelve ounce NY Strip, which included chef's potatoes. The squiggly things are fried shallots. You have tomato confit and sauce au poivre. Polo, we have more than enough food on this table to eat."

"Look at our main courses. They are kid's portions. Maneee, I'mma be hungry soon as I stand up," he stated before sighing heavily and shaking his head.

Laughing, I shook my head before demanding him to eat his food. Without further ado, that hood nigga began eating his food while shaking his head.

"So, how do you like the squiggly things?" I asked in a joking manner.

"Them lil' worm things ain't that bad," he voiced before shoving the last of the fried shallots into his mouth.

Our main courses went by quickly. Then, we tackled the appetizers along with our drinks. The soft music and dim lighting set the mood in the restaurant, further causing us to relax and talk.

"So, tell me why you aren't in a relationship, Cella?"

"Just don't feel like dealing with the lies and bullshit. I've only been in three serious relationships, and those dudes weren't ready for a woman like me," I told him as I grabbed a couple pieces of cubed cheese.

"Are you an' yo' baby daddy fresh out of a relationship?"

"No. I broke things off with him when Xyla turned two. Xyla's my heart, you know, and I wasn't up for him trying to down play our child. I saw myself doing something to him; therefore, I knew he had to go. He wasn't worth me going to prison."

Silence overcame us as Polo glared into my face. The way he looked at me caused me to squirm in the warm, comfortable seat. My body became warm as I studied his posture, facial structure, and the beautiful artwork plastered on his arms.

After clearing my throat, I said, "So, what is your relationship status like?"

"I'm single. I do or did have a broad that I kick it with from time to time. I haven't been in a serious relationship since my twin sons mother. By the way, which was back in the day."

"Hmm. The chick that you kick it with from time to time is she the chick that came into the store?"

"Yeah."

Nodding my head, I chose not to address the two-way answer he gave me about whether they were kicking it.

"Are you ready to go?" he asked before licking his lips.

"Yes. Are you ready to turn it in fo' the night?" I inquired as I realized that I hadn't talked to Xyla since earlier today.

I gotta call her before she goes to bed, I thought as I grabbed my purse.

While I retrieved my wallet, he replied, "No, I'm not ready to turn it in. Are you?"

"No," I answered as I signaled for our waitress to come over.

"Why do you have yo' wallet out? I hope you don't think you are payin' fo' our meals," he voiced seriously in an oh so sexy tone.

"Yes, I am paying for dinner. You got me next go round, right?" I asked sweetly.

"Nawl, you got us next. I got us this time."

Sighing heavily, I said, "I suggested the place; thus, I pay. Don't argue with me, Polo. No, I am not flexing on you or anything. No, I am not trying to show you that I can take care of myself. I just wanted to treat you to something different. I want to be something different towards and for you even if we are just friends. So, don't fight me on this one."

"You win, woman," he stated before chuckling.

"Since neither of us are ready to call it a night ... What are we gonna do next?"

"Walk down by the riverboat, watch movies, play cards, anything," I voiced as the waitress approached the table.

"That's what's up."

It was approaching nine o'clock p.m.; thus, I told Polo that I had to make a call to my little lady. Nodding his head, he sat back and watched me interact with my daughter on the phone. She boasted about her day with her grandparents and cousins.

The huge smile my child had on her face was what I lived for, day and night. It was the best feeling a woman could have besides having an orgasm. The moment the waitress appeared at the table with the receipt, I sweetly and lovingly ended the call with Xyla.

After I paid her in cash along with a tip, Polo stood with a frown on his face and said, "I know damn well that lil' ass meal we had didn't equal out to be a hunnid an' fifty somethin' dollars."

Standing, I announced, "Yep. They are expensive; yet, they are just that damn good to pay that price."

"Shit. We could've made that damn meal at my crib an' still bought som' other type of groceries," he stated as I handed him the keys to Tealy.

While we stepped away from the table, he asked, "Oh, so you gonna let me whip Tealy again, huh?"

"Yep. I feel like being chauffeured around for a change."

"That's what' up," he replied as he opened the restaurant's door for me.

Stepping into the humid air, I exhaled and inhaled several times. The different aromas of food being prepared were always a delight to inhale.

"Do you want to drive towards the riverfront or walk?" he asked me, breaking my observance of the atmosphere.

"We can drive. I'm sure we are going to get some drinks while we around other eateries," I responded coolly.

"A'ight," he replied as he unlocked my car doors.

I thought he was going to hop in the driver's seat, but he didn't. He opened the passenger door for me. Feeling bubbly inside, I sweetly thanked him. Never had I ever had a dude, beside my dad that opened a car door for me. So, of course, I felt some type of way, and it wasn't a bad feeling—at all.

As Polo rounded the front of Tealy, I unlocked and opened the driver's door for him.

The moment his ass took a seat in my car, he looked at me with a mischievous grin plastered on his handsome face before saying, "Oh, I love this damn whip. I see myself drivin' it long term."

"Oh, really?" I piped.

"Yep, an' ain't shit you can say 'bout that huh?"

"Not a damn thing."

"And you bet not eitha," he seriously stated while looking at me as he placed the key into the gold ignition.

"Yes, sir." I chuckled as I saluted him.

"You are so damn silly woman. Let's enjoy the rest of our night." He smiled at me and I swore I saw fireworks exploding.

Lord, please let things go smoothly between the two of us. I'm digging Polo, I thought as he reversed my whip.

CHAPTER NINE
Polo

Monday, June 4th

Bam. Bam. Bam.

The loud thunderous knocks sounded off at my back door. Cella wiggled in my arms as I pried my eyes open.

Bam. Bam. Bam.

"I know your ass in there Polo! So, open this damn door!" Joana yelled while she continued to bam on my fucking door as if she was twelve.

Cella looked at me with a blank facial expression before lifting the covers off her.

Mane, let me go get this chick from my place, I thought as I jumped out of the bed.

Hopping down the seventeen stairs, I was angry as hell. I didn't like being disturbed out of my sleep for some bullshit. I was sleeping comfortably with Cella in my arms, in my bed — after staying up half the night drinking, laughing, and watching movies.

As I unlocked my doors, the crazy broad was going off. The moment I opened the door, shawty tried her best to step her ass into my home.

"Nawl, guh, I ain't tell yo' ass to step foot in my shit. What in the fuck is wrong wit' you? Comin' by a nigga spot an' shit. You know I don't play that. If I didn't call yo' motherfuckin' ass over here, why in the fuck is you here?" I asked in an annoyed, stern timbre.

"I wanna know who is the bitch you had all over town yesterday and last night? You must forgot we an item or some shit?" she hissed while rolling her neck and shoving a long, acrylic nail in my face.

Chuckling at the disturbed broad, I hit her ass with a nasty response that sent her ass overboard. Not the one to argue with a bitch that doesn't understand simple English, I closed the door in her face. Why in the fuck did I do that? That broad showed her ass by calling my momma while she was standing at my fucking front door.

"Well, you have your hands full this morning, huh?" Cella laughed as her beautiful tail sauntered down the stairs wearing one of my black T-shirts.

As I shook my head, I sighed heavily followed by saying, "Shit crazy."

Cocking her head to the left, Cella looked at me in a way that made my knees buckle. I wanted badly to snatch her in my arms and rain kisses on her face. I badly wanted to feel her insides. I badly wanted to know did she taste as sweet as she looked and smelled.

"Why are you lookin' at me like that, woman?" I asked as I heard my cell phone ringing, followed by Joana shouting that Karma was going to get me.

"No reason," Cella replied before stretching.

"What do you have planned fo' today?" I asked, hoping that she didn't have anything planned.

"Nothing, actually. I'm off on Monday's. Unless, there is a client that needs artwork ranging from three hundred dollars and higher," she confessed before nibbling on her bottom lip.

As I replied cool, thunder sounded off causing Cella to jump.

Laughing, I said, "Oou, somebody scared."

Rolling her eyes, she responded with a smile on her face, "Shut up, Polo, and you better not tell a soul either."

"Your secret is safe wit' me," I voiced as I ambled towards her.

Last night and this morning was my first time having a woman in my crib — in my bed — and I didn't have my dick inside of them. As bad as I wanted to spread Cella's legs, I didn't. I understood what she went through in the past, and I sure as hell respected her as a woman.

Thunder sounded off again causing Cella to run her ass up the stairs.

"I know damn well yo' ass ain't runnin' from no thunder, woman." I laughed as I jogged up the stairs.

As I stood on the last step and looked towards my bed, Cella's ass was underneath the covers still as a mouse caught in a cat's mouth. Her beautiful eyes were big as the thunder rumbled.

I couldn't help but laugh at her ass. It was cute seeing her afraid of thunder.

"Are you hungry?" I asked as I took a seat on the bed.

"Yes," she replied as her phone rang.

"What do you want to eat?"

With her phone in her hand, she announced lowly, "Whatever you fix, I'll eat."

"Cool," I responded as she answered her phone at the same time my phone sounded off.

By the way she talked on the phone, I knew it was one of her homegirls on the line. I ignored my phone as I skipped down the stairs. Once I landed on the last step, knocks sounded at my back door.

Sighing heavily, I spat, "Joana take yo' ass home!"

"This isn't Joana, nigga," Janah spat nastily.

What in the fuck is she doin' here? Who in the fuck told this bitch where I live? I thought as I snatched my gun from the table and ensured that I had a round in the chamber.

Coming close towards the door, I said, "What do you want?"

"It's raining hard, Polo. Open the door, please," she begged.

Snatching the door open with my gun displayed, I looked at the one woman that I used to care so deeply for and spat, "What?"

"May I come in?" she asked as I saw the rain dancing sideways while a gust of wind swirled wet paper debris around the parking lot.

"Nawl, speak," I told her roughly before a series of thunder noises sounded off.

I knew that Cella was in my bed scared shitless which caused me to quickly rush whatever Janah wanted out of her mouth, so that I could give her my one-on-one attention.

"Your sons and I are homeless. We need somewhere to stay, Polo," she voiced as her eyes became watery.

Laughing, I replied, "Where that nigga at that you ran off wit'? Wit' my fuckin' money at that. Where that new nigga at? You better go to those niggas an' ask them fo' a place to stay. Yo' ass got some nerves poppin' up at my shit askin' fo' help. Bitch, are you crazy? As far as my boys, you know they can come live wit' me. Yo' ass ain't welcomed at all. I give no fucks 'bout you!"

"Polo, my boys aren't staying if I can't."

"Where are they?" I asked, trying to conceal my anger.

"That's none of your business." She shot back with an attitude.

"Now, what kind of shit is this, Janah? You tell me that you an' my boys are homeless. Yet, you won't tell me where they are. I'm goin' to ask yo' ass one time an' one time only ...where in the fuck are my sons?"

"Are you goin' to let us live with you or are you going to put us in our own home?" she asked, clearly ignoring my questions.

The look on my face was priceless as I slammed the door in her damn face followed by taking three steps into the kitchen. I didn't know who in the fuck she thought I was, but I wasn't a sucker for her pretty, evil ass anymore. She could kiss my ass for all I cared. There wasn't a way in hell I was bringing Janah into my home. She stole from me once her ass would do it again.

As I sighed sharply, I shook my head at the bullshit Janah presented me. While looking through the refrigerator, I had to stop myself from thinking about Janah and how badly I hated her. I didn't need her ass fucking up my day with some scheming shit. Focusing on breakfast, I decided that I would cook boneless pork chops, hash browns, eggs, grits, and pancakes. While I whipped the most important meal of the day, my mind tried telling me there was a better way that I could have handled the situation; that was until I thought about how I always fell weak for that conniving bitch. Janah had schemed me enough — from the first day I placed my eyes on her ass.

Breakfast was done by the time Cella waltzed down the stairs.

"Umm, it smells good down here," she voiced lightly.

"Thanks. Now, what would you like to drink?"

"Do you have orange juice and wine?" she asked while taking a seat at my kitchen table.

"Yes," I replied with a frown on my face.

"Good. I will make us a mimosa."

"I see yo' ass love alcohol," I stated as I placed food onto black, square plates.

"Indeed."

For the next thirty minutes, we enjoyed our food, drinks, and conversation. The vibe between us was just right—just like Janah and my vibe in the beginning of our relationship.

What if Cella try to pull som' slick shit on me? What if I fall head over heels into my feelin's wit' her an' she gives me her ass to kiss? What if she begins to throw up how much money she makes versus me? There is no way that she is really this chill an' trill.

As question after question slammed into my mental, I began to place that brick wall up. Noticing what I was doing, I quickly told myself that I needed to cut my shit short and to never bring my past relationship into whatever Cella and I would have or try to have.

"Are you okay?" Cella asked as she placed her hand on top of mine.

Looking at her I wanted to say yes, but I felt the oddest thing causing me to tell her the truth.

"No, I'm not."

"Why?"

Sighing heavily, I replied, "Believe it or not, I was hurt by my twin sons' mother. She was the reason I shut my feelin's down an' only kicked it wit' a female or seven ... intentionally not makin' them mine. Soon as they caught feelin's an' shit, I kicked them to the curb. I wasn't up fo' gettin' hurt again."

As I connected our hands together, I continued, "I gotta be honest, Cella, I like you. You trill, chill, got yo' head an' shit togetha. You are rare. A woman that has the same interests as a man ... very rare. We have so much in common 'til it's sort of scary. I would like to get to know you better ... if you are willin' to get to know me better but we can't rush shit."

Nodding her head, she sweetly chuckled, "I thought we got that established at the lake house that we would get to know each other better.

"We did. Just had to let it be known again."

With a smile on her face, she goofily replied, "Roger that, sir."

Shaking my head while chuckling, I voiced, "Wit' that bein' said ... I need you to be upfront wit' me at all times. Don't lie or sugarcoat shit wit' me. Just be one hunnid. Understood?"

"Understood, and I expect the same thing from you," she announced with a serious expression on her beautiful face.

Being a man of my word and honoring what we agreed upon, I boldly said, "Cella, I wanna know do you taste as sweet as you smell and look."

Throwing her head back and giggling, she hit a nigga with, "If things go well between us, you shall find out."

***

Cella was on the phone chopping it up with Xyla. The look she had on her face as she was comfortably posted on her grey and red sectional at the lake house was absolutely breathtaking. I couldn't keep my eyes off her as she talked with her daughter. I loved seeing women interact with their children. That maternal bonding between a woman and her child was everything to me.

"Damn, y'all got this kitchen stinkin' somethin' awful. I'm so damn ready to eat," Russ stated as he grabbed a pitcher of some concoction that Cella made.

It was the ladies idea to cook dinner for us. I couldn't lie those freaky friends of Cella's could cook their asses off. Each one had a special niche when it came down to food. Sunny was big on eating healthy; thus, she prepared a mean ass Greek salad with all the trimmings that had some funny, crumbly looking as cheese called Feta. Ke'Lena cooked cabbages with chopped ham hock pieces, cornbread, and a pineapple cheesecake which Cella infused with Skyy Vodka. Tyanna whipped up parmesan and spinach stuffed chicken breast and yellow rice for the side. Vanice cooked meatloaf with homemade mashed potatoes.

Crystal fixed a crab boil. Shanice prepared cubed steak and gravy, and Cella's ass was over the liquor infused fruit and dessert. I couldn't lie as if I wasn't impressed with the way those women worked the kitchen after participated in a fuckathon—majority of the weekend.

"Xyla, I will come by to see you before I go to work. Okay, sweetie?" Cella's beautiful voice spoke from the living room.

"Me love you more, Duda Byrd. Sleep tight my beautiful princess. Tell my Momma and Daddy I said goodnight and I love them," Cella cooed before she waltzed into the kitchen with a warm look on her face.

Placing her phone on the counter, she asked, "Where am I needed?"

"On som' dick like we been half of the weekend," Ke'Lena and Vanice spat in unison, causing me to spit out the alcohol I had in my mouth.

"Well, shit, then," my niggas spat as I laughed.

As we laughed at the comment, Cella sauntered towards the dessert and fruit table laughing before telling Ke'Lena and Vanice, "Y'all really make me sick."

"Too many cobwebs on that lil' pussy," Crystal stated, resulting in us not ceasing our laughter.

"You ain't gotta do me like that, Crystal," Cella snickered while placing fruit on a small sturdy paper plate.

"Mane, y'all need to run all that food to the tables outside. Shit, I can't take the aroma no damn mo'," Ponytail stated seriously as the rest of us, fellas, chimed in.

Twenty minutes later, we were sitting on the back porch as we feasted on the lovely food that the ladies prepared. I tried everything, and I wasn't disappointed at all! I went back for seconds and so did my niggas. Once dinner was over with, we let our food settle before we gobbled the alcohol infused dessert and fruit.

By the time I ate my fifth pineapple and tenth damn strawberry I was fucked up beyond repair.

"Mane, what in the fuck is in those damn fruits an' desserts, Cella. I'm throwed than a motherfucka," Gwap spat as he slumped back in the comfortable lounge chair.

"Moonshine," Cella stated with a smile on her face.

"What the fuck!" we stated in unison as she laughed.

"You got us fucked up off that damn moonshine," Big sang before laughing.

As we laughed at that fool, my cell phone rang. Fumbling and bumbling to get it off the holster, I was on the verge of saying fuck the call when I noticed my niggas phones were ringing as well. The only time our shit sounded off like that was when something major has popped off.

"Nih, who in the fuck in jail now?" Dame questioned in an agitated timbre as we answered our phone.

"Hello," I voiced after I answered my mother's call.

"Son, where are you?" she asked as if she had been crying.

Before I could tell her where I was at, my niggas said, "Ahh, shit! Ahh, shit!"

Instantly, the ladies stopped talking and laughing and focused on us.

"At a friend's house. Gwap, Ponytail, Russ, Big, VJ, an' Dame got a call also. What's wrong, Momma?" I asked as I sat upright, looking at my niggas as they shook their heads with a sad facial expression.

My mother sighed heavily as Gwap and Ponytail waltzed behind me.

"Son, Madison Junior and Jonah are dea--," she stated before I cut her off.

"Momma, you better not tell me that my damn twin sons are not on this damn earth no mo'. Don't sit on this phone an' tell me no shit like that. Momma, you trippin. My boys ain't dead!"

I spat as I felt my heart breaking as my soul damn near left my body.

The ladies gasped, "Oh, my God."

Cella was gently rubbing my back as my mother softly told me the worst words a parent could ever speak to their child on behalf of their grandchildren.

"I'm sorry, Madison. They were in a horrible accident with Janah this morning around nine-thirty ... somewhere in Montgomery. Janah died at the scene. Jonah and Madison Junior died at the hospital around eleven-thirty," she sobbed as I overheard my father in the background.

I couldn't handle what my mother told me on top of knowing that I closed the door on Janah. The thought of Janah coming to my house to ask for living assistance tugged at my core. The rehashing of me being nasty to Janah caused a low ugly growl to escape. The image of me slamming my front door in her face because she wouldn't tell me where my boys were caused me to lash out. The whole fucking time my boys were in the car with her.

Everything on the table and my phone were on the ground in a matter of seconds.

"Not my fuckin' boys!" I yelled as Ponytail grabbed me into a strong embrace.

"Not my fuckin' boys!" I cried.

I sank to the ground as my niggas and the ladies surrounded me. The cries that left my mouth were foreign to me. I felt like a bitch as I cried like it was nobody's business. Yet, I couldn't pull myself together.

"They would be here if I hadn't closed that motherfuckin' door in Janah's face. They wouldn't be lyin' in an ugly ass, cold morgue. Them not bein' here is my fuckin' fault," I cried as I felt Cella's soft hands wrapping around me.

"Cuz, this isn't yo' fault," Gwap stated sadly as the others agreed with him.

"It is! I closed the door in her face today when she told me that her an' my boys were homeless! I told her my sons could stay but she couldn't. If I … if I … what kind of man am I to tell her that she couldn't stay at my home wit' our sons?" I cried out.

Cella shoo'd me as she rocked our bodies.

Gently pushing her off me, I said, "I gotta go."

"I'm goin' to ride wit' you," the fellas chimed in as I shook my head.

"Then, I will ride with you," Cella offered with sadness in her eyes.

"I don't want you to go eitha," I told her in a stern tone before walking to my car with hurt and hatred in my heart as I refused to let another tear drop down my face.

CHAPTER TEN
Cella

Tuesday, June 5th

"Thanks for hooking me up, Cella. You are truly the best," another satisfied customer stated before leaving my work space.

"No problem, love. I'm very glad that you love your leg artwork," I stated sweetly as I cleaned my work station.

"You have a great evening and night."

"Same to you, sweetie."

The moment my client left my work area, I sighed heavily as I was thankful for the end of the work day. It was super busy. The walk-in customers overpowered me today. Normally, I wouldn't mind but today my heart, soul, and mind wasn't into tattooing. I had been worried about Polo. Ever since he left the lake house last night, he had been on my mind — heavily.

Before I came to work and during lunch, I stopped by the shop and went by his home to check on him. He wasn't at either place. Of course, I had to call VJ and ask him have he talked to Polo, and he said yes. Immediately, I felt some type of way.

"Hey, are you okay?" Shanice asked sweetly as she waltzed into my work area.

"Not really. Polo isn't answering any phone calls from me. I'm worried about him."

"He just needs some time to process things. Trust, he'll come around."

Nodding my head, I replied, "Yeah, you are right."

"Russ told me that he's taking it real hard."

"I know," I voiced softly as we exited my work station.

While talking about Polo and the loss of his twin sons, Shanice and I made sure that my place was up to par before we left.

"Chat tonight?" she asked after I locked my establishment.

"Oh, so you, Sunny, Tyanna, Crystal, and Ke'Lena aren't doing word count challenges tonight? Now, I know hell is going to freeze over if y'all ain't writing tonight." I laughed.

"Oh, we beating them keys up tonight but not before we have our girls chat about the niggas we was with this weekend," Shanice voiced in a naughty manner.

Rolling my eyes, I jokingly said, "I do not want to hear about y'all's fuck sessions. Polo and I heard everything y'all nasty ass said and did."

"Well, shouldn't your little cobwebbed pussy be sore."

"You know what?"

"What?" she laughed.

"After I put Xyla to bed, I will call you and we will plug the others in because I know y'all asses are dying to tell me what y'all nasty asses really did."

"Wait ... what do you mean by spend time with Xyla? The deal was for you to not interrupt her summer and that she was going to stay with your parents the *entire* summer, Cella. What made you change your mind?"

"Seeing Polo distraught over his sons' death had me wanting to hold Xyla in my arms for the night. Thus, I told my parents why I wanted to have her home. They understood and told me that I was only keeping her for one night," I voiced casually as images of Polo losing it after the horrible news was revealed to him over the phone.

"Yeah, I was ready to have my son with me also."

"So, you understand where I'm coming from?"

"Absolutely. No more flaking out on our pre-planned kid-free summer."

"Never."

"Okay. Tell your parents I said hello."

"I will when I call them."

"Um, aren't you going to get Xyla from their home?"

"Honey, no. That spoiled child saw my brother at Wal-Mart and left with him ... as she held onto six bags filled with clothes and toys."

"I swear that child loves shopping more than me," Shanice stated while shaking her head.

"Yep."

After we hugged and kissed each other on the cheek, we hopped in our cars and smashed out. The ride to my brother's house wasn't far from my business. I made it there in no time. As soon as I pulled my Range Rover in my brother's driveway, Xyla rushed out of the door with her small suitcase and a huge smile on her face as my brother wasn't too far behind her.

"Hi, Mommy," my beautiful little one voiced as she wrapped her long arms around my waist.

"Hey, baby. How was your day?" I asked her before greeting my brother.

"It was good and funny. Uncle Joshua burnt the cookies."

"See what had happened was," my thirty-five year old brother voiced before laughing.

"Let me guess, you forgot the cookies were in the oven," I stated while shaking my head.

"Sis, you do know me don't it? I forgot. Plus, Roxy's ugly shaggy ass has been shittin' all over the house. I'm 'bout ready to put som' anti-freeze in the bitch's dog food," he said in an annoyed yet funny tone.

"Boy, you better not do nothing to that damn dog you had for seven years." I laughed as I pictured my brother fussing at his beautiful French Bull dog for pooping in his crib.

"Little fucker better stop shittin' all over my floors," he stated in an agitated tone.

"Uncle Joshua, has the vet called you yet?" Xyla questioned.

"No. They have less than ten minutes to call me before Roxy is placed on the side of the road."

Shaking my head, I dismissed Xyla to the car so that I could talk to my brother in a grown up manner.

"Joshua, my back is up against the wall when it comes down to LaJuan doing right by Xyla. I'm trying my best not to have full custody of her. What more can I do?"

Sighing heavily, my wise no children having brother said, "There's nothing that you can do. He doesn't want to be involved Cella. No need in stressin' over a nothin' ass nigga that doesn't see his blessin' that he has created."

"So, I need to follow through with the custody thing?"

"Yep. Cella, it ain't like the nigga ever did anythin' fo' her besides lie to her. Between mom, dad, Traneice, an' me we have her when you are workin' anyways."

"True."

"I'm surprised you hadn't been stripped that nigga's rights away."

"I didn't want to seem bitter."

"Fuck seemin' bitter. You would be doin' the right thing fo' you an' Xyla. Trust, Cella, I see yo' patience is runnin' thin wit' him. The only reason I hadn't stepped in 'cause you made me promise that I wouldn't slaughter the nigga."

After staring at my brother for some time, I nodded my head followed by saying, "Well, I guess that it that. It's time for me to set my child free from him."

"Thatta girl," my brother voiced as he pulled me in for a hug.

"Thanks for letting her tag with you today.

"No problem."

"How much did you spend on her today?"

"Now, that little sister is none of yo' business."

"And why is that?" I laughed.

"Because somethin' is tellin' me that you are tryin' to pay me back 'cause I bought my niece some things?

"Because I am," I replied seriously.

"How many times will we have to tell you to stop throwin' money at us when it comes down to Xyla? We are not Traneice, Cella. Our parents an' I have money so stop askin' an' sneakin' money into our dresser drawers; however, we do like those little doodle notes you leave. I'm serious, Cella," he voiced sternly while glaring into my teary eyes.

"I can't help it. I guess I don't want y'all to feel that I'm taking advantage of y'all watching Xyla while I work," I stated as a tear slipped down my face.

"Dude, shut all that punk ass shit up. The only person worried 'bout some money is our greedy, triflin' ass baby sister."

"Mmhm," I agreed as I wiped my eyes.

If our sister found a way to make money without clocking into someone else's job, the lazy broad was all over the gig. Traneice wasn't career-goal oriented; she wanted things handed to her. She was the youngest, and boy, did it show when Joshua and I were around her.

"Thanks for chatting with me, Joshua. A sister is tied boss ... time for me to take it in for the night," I spoke as I made my way towards the driver's door as my brother made his way to the passenger side.

After we issued out our 'see you later's' and 'I love you's', Xyla and I aimed for our home. Per usual, Xyla engaged us in an interesting conversation that led to other conversations. By the time we made it home, we were on another topic concerning her latest infatuation with becoming a YouTube vlogger. Of course, I told her okay. The moment I agreed, she had a thousand things she wanted to talk about — concerning the YouTube gig.

Dinner went by smoothly, even though my baby was still talking about being a vlogger. Once dinner ended, we played ten rounds of Go Fish. I must say that she beat me. I couldn't get more than three matches for nothing.

Every time she asked for a number and I had it, she would yell out, "Yea, I'm the best in this game."

At eight-thirty p.m., she was sound asleep in her bed. Normally, I would kiss her on the forehead and escape out of her room but this time I laid in the bed with her. As I held her tightly, I said a prayer over her followed by praying for Polo and his family.

Closing Xyla's bedroom door, I heard my cell phone ringing. I prayed like hell it was Polo calling me. I needed him to know that I was here for him. I needed him to know that he could confide in me.

As I rushed to the living room, I damn near tripped on an ugly ass doll limb.

Rolling my eyes, I nastily stated, "I'm so tired of Xyla pulling these damn doll limbs off. Like what's the purpose in me buying these motherfuckers if she going to do them that way. Shit."

My phone stopped ringing only to start back again. As I scooped it off the end table, my heart raced as a smile spread across my face.

"Hello," I voiced while taking a seat on my sofa.

"What's up, Cella?" Polo stated in a drunken manner.

"Good. I don't feel right asking you how are you doing because I know the answer. Thus, I'm going to ask you are you able to drive to my house?"

"Yeah," he spoke in a slurred tone.

"I tell you what … I don't feel comfortable with you driving while being drunk. I will come and get you."

"Nawl, that ain't necessary. I'm already out and about anyways. What's your address?"

I gave him my address. He tried his best to get off the phone with me, but I wouldn't let him. We didn't say a word as he drove to my house. It was apparent that Future's song "Sorry" was on repeat. The song was one of my favorite songs, but at that moment I couldn't bob my head along to the mellow, bombastic beat. Why? Because I knew that there was a reason for Polo to have the song on repeat, and it was a no brainer that it had a lot to do with the death of his sons after a conversation went wrong with their mother.

Twenty-five minutes later, Polo said, "I'm outside."

"Okay," I voiced as I hopped away from my sofa.

My heart was racing out of my chest as I was eager to embrace him. I was eager to rub on him so that his mind would ease— somewhat. I wanted him to be in the presence of someone that would be there for him in his time of need.

"I'm all fucked up, Cella," he voiced in a slurred manner as he staggered into my home.

"I know, Polo, I know. Come in and make yourself at home," I told him as I closed and locked my door.

"You have a nice home," he voiced as he sauntered into my living room.

"Thank you," I replied quickly before continuing, "Would you like anything to eat or drink ... non-alcohol?"

"Nawl, I'm good," he responded as he plopped down on my sofa, glaring at me.

Taking a seat next to him, I delicately rubbed the back of his hands. I knew he didn't want to hear me say that everything was going to be ok or that his sons were in a better place. I was sure that he heard those phrases enough. Thus, I sat beside him and let him be quiet.

Kicking off his shoes, Polo was quiet and distant. It seemed as if he was dealing with more than just the death of his children. I observed him as he closed his eyes and shook his head.

"Am I dreamin'?" he asked aloud.

I remained silent. I sure as hell wasn't going to say no. That was the last thing that I felt that he needed to hear.

"Cella, they were good boys. They were smart kids. They loved that science shit. I really thought that they would become employed by NASA. They were just that damn smart," he announced before chuckling.

Continuing, he said, "Those boys loved their sisters. Junior and Jonah swore they were the oldest. They wouldn't let any boys talk to their eleven and thirteen years old sisters. They were their protectors."

For the next hour and half, I listened to Polo talk about his children—mostly about the twins. I felt his pain. I felt that he was slipping away. I felt that he needed to be hugged tightly, and I did just that.

"Cella, how in the fuck am I supposed to overcome this ... hurt ... pain?" he questioned as his voice broke down.

"By having your family and friends there to help you," I told him as I gently massaged his back.

Passionately massaging my thighs and lower back, Polo began kissing on my neck. As he placed perfect, moist kisses on my neck, I cooed at the softness of his lips. I wished that I could allow the kisses to continue but I had to stop what was taking place.

"Polo, this isn't the best time for us to be engaging in anything sexual," I told him softly as my loving box began to wake up.

"I disagree," he voiced from the crook of my neck.

It took everything in me to move my neck away from his mouth. When I did, I sternly looked at him.

Softly, I spoke, "We are not going to do this, Polo. Lay in my lap and rest your mind."

Without hesitation, he did what I said as he sighed heavily. Young Thug's "Best Friend" played on my phone. Instantly, I knew it was one of my girls. Polo lifted his head off my lap but I told him that my phone would be alright. As he placed his head back onto my thighs, my heart was breaking at the sight of a strong, African American man that loved his children from the pits of his loins. My heart went out to him as he had to prepare himself to bury two of his children as he had to deal with telling their mother that she couldn't live at his home. My heart split in half at the thought of how he was mentally tearing himself down.

Before I knew it, tears ran down my face as I placed a kiss on the top of Polo's head all the while saying a special prayer for him.

***

I was awakened out of my sleep by a sudden, forceful urge to loudly moan as my body shook uncontrollably. Glad that I realized that my daughter was two doors away from me, I popped my eyes open only to see Polo's face stuffed between my legs — feasting on my loveliness with such passion. Quickly, I realized why I denied him access before we came to my room for R&R while watching T.V.

Sighing and moaning at the same time, I tried moving my body. I failed miserably as Polo clamped his warm, wet mouth on my clit and gently yet savagely sucked on it. Slowly snaking two fingers inside of my hole, Polo groaned while tasting every ounce of me. I loved the way he took his time sucking and licking every drop of juice my body provided him.

"Polo, we ... shouldn't ... be," I stammered as one of his fingers tapped on my G-Spot and another danced in an area that had me gripping the back of his head.

"You taste just as good as you smell and look," he groaned while massaging my thigh with his left hand.

My back arched as I lowly cooed his name. Tears seeped down my face as my body felt as if it was on fire. Knowing that we shouldn't be engaging in sexual activities, I gave him the nut that he was seeking. I allowed him to suck life out of me only to return it back. My highs came down and I knew I had to pull away before we had sex—something neither of us was truly ready for.

"Polo, we need to stop. Come on and lay by me. Let's talk," I told him as he looked at me with hungry, lustful eyes.

Removing his mouth from my loveliness, he shook his head followed by saying, "Yo' pussy an' I are talkin'. My fingers an' yo' pussy are talkin'. So, lay back an' let them continue to talk."

I didn't have a dog in that fight. He dominated me in a way that left me speechless. All I could do was cum, moan, and have lifeless limbs as he brought me to multiple orgasms — something no man has ever brought me.

Going against my better judgment, I cooed, "Polo, I want to feel you."

"Okay," he responded as he finished drinking my sweet extract.

As he retrieved a condom from the back pocket of his jeans, I felt edgy as I knew that I was rusty in the sex department. While Polo placed the condom on his thick, long dick, I tried to steady my breathing by exhaling and inhaling slowly. That shit didn't work!

"Cella," Polo sexily growled as he took his jeans off.

"Yes," I skittishly replied.

"I want you," he replied sternly as he climbed in between my shaky legs.

"I want you too," I uttered as he circled the head of his dick on my clit.

I hated to admit it, but the condom was ruining the moment. Yet, we weren't in a position to be having raw sex—hell sex period. I didn't know him that well to engage in no-protection sexual acts.

As Polo inserted the head of his dick inside of me, I winced.

"You good, bae?" he whispered in my ear before sucking on my earlobe.

Lying, I replied, "Yes."

Gently thrusting into my loveliness, Polo grunted before saying, "How long has it really been since you had sex, Cella?"

With an awkward look on my face, I announced, "Four years."

Bringing his face to mine, glaring into my eyes, he asked, "Are you serious right nih?"

While nodding my head, I responded, "Yes."

With a blank facial expression, Polo licked and sucked on my bottom lip as he tried inching his dick inside of me. For fifteen minutes, we tried our damnedest to get things going the right way. However, my pussy had other things in mind—not having sex with a condom on. I wasn't up for that but Polo was. In a swift move, he took the condom off and slipped his fat, chocolatey dick head inside of my tight loveliness.

"Ooou," I whined as I felt my body relaxing to his naked dick.

My legs open more, eager to receive him. The feeling of his thick veins throbbing and pulsating inside of me caused my loveliness to become moist—which the condom had taken some of my juices away. Inch by inch, Polo stroked me in a way that had me eager to satisfy the inches that were stuffed inside of me. Wall to wall, roof to bottom of my pussy was filled to capacity. That damn man had a dick that would make a bitch obey—even if he was in the wrong.

We found the perfect rhythm and went for what we knew. The passionate sounds that left our mouths were blissful. The clenching of our bodies was life for me. Him whispering thank you for being a friend to me had my heart on swollen mode. Him knocking down every fucking cobweb in my loveliness sent me over the edge.

As we sexed each other something good, my bedroom door opened. The look on my face was priceless as I saw Xyla rubbing her eyes as Polo had my legs over his shoulders with his dick in my lovely hole. My face was red as Polo's was a shade darker.

"Mommy, what is you--," Xyla stated as Polo and I scrambled to get out of a non-child viewing position.

I didn't know what to say other than. "Xyla, honey, would you like a juice or snack or something?"

As she nodded her head while rubbing her eyes, my beautiful daughter sauntered out of the room. I had to dress, quickly. I looked at Polo, and I was frightened at the facial expression that he had—emotionless.

"Polo," I called out.

"Yeah," he replied with zero feelings.

"Do you want anything from the kitchen?"

"Nawl, I'm good."

"Okay. I'll be right back. I gotta get her situated."

"A'ight."

Ten minutes later, I had Xyla in her room and I was back in mine—locked in. I was eager to pick things up between Polo and me. However, he was dressing all the while shaking his head.

"Talk to me, Polo," I begged him as I stood in front of him.

"There's nothin' to talk 'bout, Cella. I gotta go. I'll lock the door behind me," he replied inexpressively as he dashed past me.

Feeling as if I was just played like a fool, I stood and stared at my bedroom door. While glaring at my door, I hoped that he would come back and talk to me. The moment I heard my front door close, a lone tear seeped down my face. Why I felt as if I did something wrong, I don't know but I did. Questions after questions slammed in my head as I wondered what triggered Polo to shut down on me after Xyla caught us in the act.

    Finally able to find my will to climb into my large bed, I laid down with sadness all over my spirit that I couldn't shake.

CHAPTER ELEVEN
Polo

Thursday, June 7th

Ding. Ding.

With a blunt to my mouth as I held tightly onto my phone, I glared at Cella's name on the gray display screen of my phone. As I exhaled the smoke, I dropped my phone into my lap. Cella had been calling me ever since I rudely walked out on her. Not one time did I feel the need to call or text her back. I was going through something no parent should, and I didn't need her breathing down my neck every time I turned around. I wanted my space and peace.

"Aye, you good?" Big asked as he took a seat next to me in the quiet garage of our shop.

Without looking at him, I nodded my head and shoved my phone in my pocket before saying, "Yep."

"You do know we are here anytime you want to talk, right?" he continued as he fired up a blunt.

"Yep."

As we sat, getting high, my thoughts were on my boys. I couldn't get their small bodies out of my mind. I couldn't grasp the fact that I would be burying them soon. I couldn't believe that I had purchased two homegoing suits for my nine-year-old boys. It felt surreal to be dealing with some shit of this caliber. I would've preferred dealing with my teenaged daughters being pregnant than burying my boys.

"Polo," VJ called out from the back of the garage.

"Yeah," I shot back, not looking in the direction he called from.

"Aye, mane, Cella's worried 'bout you. Maybe you should give her a call," he stated while strolling towards Big and me.

"Nawl, I'm good," I replied, standing and stretching.

"Dude, she's a good woman. She's someone that you need in yo' corner right now besides us," he continued.

"Look, mane, I know she's a good woman. Yet, I don't want to deal wit' her all down my neck an' shit. I just want to be left the fuck alone. I ain't stun' no bitch, good or bad, ret nih," I nastily stated as Cella came into my eyesight.

The garage became quiet as Cella glared at me with a calm demeanor. I had zero emotions as she was in my presence. I felt nothing as her eyes were placed on me. I was—just in the wind and damn near out of control.

"Good morning, y'all," her beautiful voiced stated.

"Morning, Cella," the fellas stated as I felt the awkward tension between them and her.

I wanted to move my legs, but I couldn't. I wanted to be nasty, but I couldn't. Thus, I stood still as she strolled towards the table I was standing by. She dropped a clear plastic bag that had an orange juice bottle and a carryout plate stuffed inside.

"Wasn't sure if you had breakfast this morning or if you ate at all. I know if I was in your shoes, I wouldn't have eaten anything either. Um, once again, I'm sorry for your losses," she stated sweetly before biting down on her bottom lip as she turned on her black soles of her Fila shoes.

Like the asshole I was, I didn't say thank you. I just—stood like a fucking dummy smoking on a blunt.

"Aye, Cella, I'll be in 'round lunch time fo' that tattoo we discussed," VJ stated, breaking the ice.

"Okay. No charge on this one VJ. It's on the house."

"Now, you know I can't just not pay you."

"And you know I can't allow you to pay me when I said it's on the house." She shot back in a bossy manner.

Chuckling as he held his hands up, VJ replied, "A'ight. I ain't gon' fight you on that one."

"And you better not." She lightly laughed before continuing, "Y'all have a good day."

"Same to you," they replied as I stood there, watching her walk away—mouth sealed tighter than my blunt.

The moment her speaker knockers informed us that she was no longer in earshot, the fellas looked at me and shook their heads.

"Fuckin' dummy," they spat one by one.

"Damn fool couldn't tell that heavenly woman thank you," Ponytail stated as he shook his head at me.

Ignoring them and the nice gesture Cella did for me, I focused on a car that was assigned to me. The day went by in a blur as I didn't focus on anything other than the car that had to be out of the garage and in the care of its owner by five p.m. I skipped going out for lunch with the fellas, but I did eat the delicious upscale breakfast Cella brought me. She truly had a unique set of taste buds.

The moment the client arrived to retrieve his car, I was eager to jet out of the door. My calm and cold crib called my name. As I breezed through the door of my home thoughts of Cella appeared. Feelings of being in the wrong of how I treated her sat at the top of my brain, causing me to pull out my phone so that I could apologize to her.

Me: *Thank you fo' bringin' me breakfast this mornin'. It was good. Aye, Cella, I'm sorry fo' how I been treated you. I'm just goin' through a lot right now that I can't explain.*

After I sent her the message, I savagely opened the refrigerator for the last beer I knew was tucked in the corner of the door. Quickly, I popped the top on it. In a matter of seconds, the bottle was empty. As I walked up the stairs, my phone vibrated and dinged. Eagerly, I pulled out my phone to see what Cella had to say. I was slightly disappointed when I saw Momma on the display screen.

Momma: *Hey, Son, we will be meeting at your father and I's home at six this evening to finish discussing the funeral arrangements for Junior and Jonah. Some of Janah's family members will be here as well. I love you, and I will see you when you get here.*

"Ugh!" I loudly stated as I climbed the steps to the bathroom.

Me: *Okay. Love you, more.*

After I replied to my mother's text, I threw my phone on the bed as I stripped naked with a severe attitude. I dreaded going to my parents' home. I didn't want to be bothered with Janah's folks. Every time I placed my eyes on them, they made my ass and index finger itch. Someone always had an input but the bitches never gave up any money. I had already laid Janah's motherfucking momma out. She wanted me to bury her daughter. There wasn't a way in hell I was going to bury that bitch. That wasn't my damn job! The fuck I looked like. My boys were all that I cared about in the situation and no one else!

Ding. Ding.

Quickly looking at my phone, I saw Cella's name displaying on the text message notification. Instantly, I retrieved my phone.

Sexy Cella: *You are welcome. Understandable.*

"That's it? That's all you gotta say?" I asked aloud as I waited to see was she going to text me something else.

Three minutes later and nothing else from Cella, I growled as I dropped the phone on the bed and made my way towards my bathroom.

"This shit is all wrong. From my kids dyin' to me an' Cella," I stated in an annoyed tone as I turned the water knobs on.

While I showered, my cellphone and doorbell dinged. Not giving a damn about either of them, I continued cleaning my body. The moment I hopped out of the shower, I waltzed into my walk-in closet. Quickly, I retrieved an-all black attire and the latest jewelry that I purchased from the Arabs jewelry store in Eastdale Mall.

Thirty minutes later, I was dressed, looking good, and smelling great. With my phone in my hand, I looked at the time; it was six fifteen p.m. I had no choice but to see the missed calls and text messages notification; however, I ignored them. Hopping down the stairs two at a time, I mentally prepared myself for the fuckery that was possibly going to pop off at my parents' crib.

Ring. Ring. Ring.

Retrieving my phone, I answered in an annoyed voice. "Yeah."

"Hey. How are you?" Joana asked softly.

"Fine."

"Do you need anything?"

"Yeah. Fo' yo' ass to stop callin' me so damn much," I nastily spat as I snatched my keys off the kitchen table.

"You don't have to be nasty to me, Polo. I'm just being a friend to you. I would've thought after th--," she stated before I cut her off.

"Who in the fuck said I needed a friend?" I growled as I opened my back door.

"You are something else, you know?"

"Yep. Nih, good damn bye," I told her before I ended the call without a care in the world of my nasty behavior towards her.

***

"All I'm saying is that Polo should contribute to Janah's funeral costs as well," Janah's mother implied as she lit a cigarette.

Laughing, I replied, "Well, you better go to her corpse, an' ask her triflin' butt where is the money she stole from me. You better do a fish fry, GoFundMe, bake sale, or somethin'. I ain't coughin' up a dime fo' her no good butt. I'm tryin' to figure out why you ain't have her in no life insurance policy to begin wit'. You knew she was a "wanna be" trap queen after all."

"That's enough, Madison. You need to go outside and get some air," my mother stated in a stern voice.

Nodding my head at the beautiful dark-skinned woman that gave birth to me, I said, "I'm goin' to head home. I think my input in the matter of my boys and Janah are heartfelt. Y'all have a good night."

Everyone one minus Janah's family said goodnight. As I skipped out of the door, I received a call from my daughters, who were on the line when I answered the phone. We chatted from the time I left my parents' home until I was halfway home. I didn't know how to feel as they were stronger than me. I didn't know how to feel hearing them say that they knew without a doubt that Junior and Jonah would be smiling down on us for the rest of their days. I was a mess by the time I pulled into the parking slot in front of my apartment's door. I needed someone to comfort me. I needed someone to kiss the top of my head while not saying a motherfucking word. I needed to feel soft arms wrapped around me as they lightly breathed on me.

With my phone in my hand, I texted Cella. She was the person that I needed.

Me: *Hey. I need you.*

Instantly, she texted back.

Sexy Cella: *"I ain't stun' no bitch, good or bad, ret nih."*

I stared at the text she sent me—the same words that I stated aloud earlier today. I felt like kicking my own ass. I was not expecting for her to throw them at me.

Me: *I didn't mean it.*

Sexy Cella: *"Yet, I don't want to deal wit' her all down my neck an' shit. I just want to be left the fuck alone." Thus, I'm doing what you want done... not being down your neck because I know you are hurting and you need someone other than your family. Oh, and I'm leaving you the fuck alone. Two in motherfucking one!*

Feeling like the dummy my niggas called me, I was. Feeling that I fucked up a cool and good thing between Cella and me, I did that.

Me: *I was dead ass wrong fo' what I said an' how I treated you. I'm sorry, Cella. I really am.*

The only thing I could do after I sincerely apologized was to sauntered my black ass towards my crib with a sad face, damaged mental, and poor spirit.

CHAPTER TWELVE
Cella

Saturday, June 9th

Out of respect, my girls and I attended the double funeral and burial for Polo's children. It was a sad, sad thing to witness. The look on that man's face as he said goodbye to his children was something that I couldn't tolerate. I couldn't imagine being in his position. I wouldn't know what to do with myself, but I knew that I wouldn't lash out on people that genuinely cared for me.

"Thank y'all fo' comin'," Polo calmly stated as we exited his parents' home—they held the repass there.

"No problem," we stated in unison as my girls hugged him while I looked off.

"You look beautiful, Cella. I love the hairstyle you are rockin," Polo stated as my girls removed themselves from him.

"Thanks," I replied as I slid my slender fingers through the blonde, long loosely curled weave that flowed beautifully on the right side of my head. I went the extra mile and had six, not small but not big stars tatted on my left temple.

"What possessed you to get the stars tatted on yo' damn head?" Russ inquired.

"Spontaneous moment, I guess," I chuckled as I was eager to leave Polo's parents' home.

Every now and again, I would do something outrageous. Last year, I had gotten my clit pierced. One too many times of getting my laced panties entangled in the damn ring thing, I took it out.

Clearing his throat, Polo said, "Cella, may I talk wit' you fo' a minute."

"No, you can't," I replied calmly yet sternly.

"Please," he begged.

Shaking my head at him, I looked at my ladies and said, "Y'all ready?"

"So, we just gonna leave without gettin' any of that delicious smelling food?" Vanice and Ke'Lena stated in a tone only we could hear in.

"Oou, y'all are too much," Tyanna spat while shaking her head as Polo laughed.

"Aren't they always too much," Dame and Big replied as they stepped out of the back door with a plate filled to capacity with food.

"I'll meet y'all at my truck," I spoke, chuckling at my greedy ass friends.

"Y'all are finna go already?" Big inquired after swallowing a mouthful of food.

"Yes," I replied as I descended the six, red steps.

"Cella," Polo called out as I waltzed to my SUV.

"Daddy!" the sweetest voices called from in front of me.

"Yes, Jalia an' Alana," Polo answered to the beautiful, tall children clothed in pretty, mourning dresses.

"Are you okay?" they asked him as I passed them with a smile on my face.

"Yes. Go in the house an' get y'all somethin' to eat. I'll be in the house soon as I chat with someone."

"Yes, sir," they replied with such obedience that lightened my heart.

"Cella," Polo called out.

Ignoring him, I was eager to sit in the driver's seat of Range Rover. I wanted to be far away from the man that I had lusted after, got in good with, and then treated like I didn't matter.

Roughly turning me around, Polo glared into my eyes before saying, "I'm really, really sorry, Cella. I ... I ...," he stated sincerely before I cut his sentence off by knocking his hand off my wrist.

I said, "You can stop saying that you are sorry. That shit doesn't move me. You spoke. I heard you. Now, we can go on about our business as if we never knew each other. No hard feelings. We weren't going to work out anyways. You are you, and I am me. With that being said, you have a good day."

"What can I do to make things right between us?" he asked as I crossed the front of my SUV.

"I'm out of your hair ... just like you wanted. I'm not breathing down your neck ... just like you wanted. You can't get more right than that, Polo."

He talked and I ignored his ass. Unlocking the doors of my vehicle, I rapidly climbed inside of my hot truck. As I started the engine, Polo was standing in front of my truck glaring at me. While I turned on the air conditioner, I didn't take my eyes off him.

My breathing became erratic as I watched his tall, strong body stand erect as his nostrils flared. The veins in his hands caused me to softly groan as I rehashed his groping hands on my body the night he left my crib without so much as a hug. Polo licked his lips as I bit my bottom lip. He mouthed that he was sorry and I shook my head.

Quickly, I looked away to see where in the hell was those friends of mine. I saw them chatting with their guys. Instantly, I grew pissed because I was ready to fucking go. I needed to be far away from Polo as possible, and their no manners asses were prolonging me from fleeing.

"These bitches think they are slick," I huffed as I retrieved my cellphone.

As I dialed Tyanna's number, Polo opened the driver's door.

"What's up, Cella?" Tyanna spoke into the phone as she looked in my direction.

"I'm ready to go," I whined as Polo massaged my thighs.

As I knocked his hands off me, Tyanna naughtily said, "It looks like you are occupied. So…"

Before I could respond to her ass, Polo voiced, "Stay, please. If you don't want to talk to me, cool, but I would love fo' you to stay. Me knowin' you are here makes a difference. Plus, the ladies don' took a seat an' I know fo' a fact they ain't ready to go."

"Welp, wit' that being said by Polo… it looks like we are staying." Tyanna laughed before ending the call.

With my mouth hanging open, I rolled my eyes at those heifers. Any other damn time, they would be on my side when I said I was going to cut a motherfucker off. Not this damn time!

I dropped my phone into the console as I looked Polo into his saddened yet mesmerizing eyes.

"Your daughters need you, don't they? I suggest you get in the house with them," I quickly spoke before being petty.

"Oops, I'm sorry ... there my ass go being down your back huh? Silly me," I stated with a not so friendly look on my face as I shut off the engine on my whip.

I was surprised that he didn't respond to my shade that I threw.

As I hopped out of my vehicle, he grabbed my left wrist, planted a kiss on it, followed by saying, "Thank you fo' stayin'."

***

"So, you gonna act like you don't see Polo calling your phone, huh?" Sunny asked as she outstretched on my sofa with her bubbly ass eyes glaring at me.

"And is," I replied before taking a sip of my lemonade moonshine.

"Um, you need to make nice," she continued as her phone rang.

"A'ight," I lied as she answered her phone all lovingly and shit.

Chuckling at my second level-headed friend, I thought about the first time I had the pleasure of meeting Sunny the paranormal, erotic, and urban fiction writer. Three and half years ago, I was at the grocery store, looking for a new type of coffee to try. This proper talking female was drilling someone out on the phone. I had to chuckle at the words and tone that she used. I knew the other person on the line felt like shit as Sunny didn't use any curse words. I could tell instantly that she was well-educated yet had a slick ass mouth.

At the end of her conversation, Sunny said, "You been staring at those coffees for a while. This is what I like. Maybe you should try it."

"Cool. Thanks," I replied before snatching the expensive yet organic coffee off the shelf.

Two weeks later, I was on the 'Book and saw a post with her book cover and photo, *Married to a Houston Bully*, on it. Instantly, I clicked on her page, sent her a friend request, followed by adding her book to my reading list. From that day forward, we had been banging hard as fuck.

"What are you doing, bookee?" Shanice asked me while taking a seat next to me at the same time Sunny escaped out the back door—giggling and shit.

"Chilling and relaxing. Trying not to think about Polo," I confessed as my phone dinged.

"So, you chilling and relaxing ain't gonna help the situation. So, why not call the man?"

"Because...," I stated, trying to not sound like a broken record.

"Because he was hurting and said some hurtful things. Okay, he did that, but he also apologized. Just hear the man out. Y'all ain't gotta get in a relationship or nothing, but I liked seeing you glowing and smiling. You deserve happiness from someone other than your parents, brother, Xyla, and us."

"True," I replied as my phone dinged again.

"Well, let me get my ass to this table and begin my word count before Russ's ass call me," she spoke happily.

"Go handle that shit, guh," I stated before blowing her an air kiss.

I had the pleasure of meeting her crazy, erotic, romance, and urban fiction ass through Sunny. Shanice was a bundle of fun with her silly ass. Not a day goes by that she doesn't have me laughing from something silly she had done, thought, or said in one of her books. She was cool and collective. Somewhat reserved but will curse a bitch out real quick.

"Aye, Shanice, what's the name of the book you just dropped not too long ago?" Sunny loudly asked from the back door.

"*Feenin' For That Dope Dick*," she replied, causing me to lightly moan.

"Okay," Sunny stated as Crystal startled the shit out of me.

"And where in the fuck did that moan come from?" Crystal asked while sauntering into the living room with her laptop bag strap slung over her right shoulder.

I couldn't answer her question because her crazy ass began patting the shit out of her head, which was covered in that damn black, silky ass bonnet that I hated so much.

"Bitccch!" I laughed as she damn near knocked her head off.

"Um, what?" she replied before looking at me crazy.

"I'mma need for you to stop slapping on your damn head like that, and why is that ugly ass bonnet on your head? I bought your ass and the others a customized damn bonnet!" I snickered as my phone dinged.

Laughing, that heifer said, "Girl, I put that pretty ass bonnet on when VJ and I get hot and heavy."

"Oh, God!" Shanice, Sunny, and I stated in unison before laughing.

"Where in the fuck did you come from, Sunny?" Crystal asked while laughing.

"I was on the patio sweet talking a bitch out of her panties," she cooed.

"Nih, what a damn minute ... I thought--," Crystal and I stated in unison before Sunny cut us off.

"Look, I'm single. Free to motherfucking mingle. Thus, I'm mingling in both worlds."

"Well, hot motherfucking damn," Crystal stated as my phone went off three times — back to back.

"Bitch, that nigga has texted you at least four times since I been standing here. Why won't you see what that man wants? Damn, let him knock those cobwebs out of that pussy. Shit," Crystal hissed before waltzing off on me, leaving me with a wide mouth and giggling broads at my kitchen table.

Shaking my head at one of the four oldest friends I had since junior high school, I thought back to the day that Crystal and I became friends. My ugly ass period had just shown face for the first time. That was the worst day of my life. Girls in my class that saw my stained white jeans joked on me. They didn't let up on my ass until Crystal, then called by her nickname Mz. Biggs, let their asses have it. Ever since then, we had been tight than a motherfucker. Not a soul could say something wrong to me without that heifer making it her business to curse a bitch out first. Crystal was a part of the writer crew as well. She was an urban fiction writer. Her latest release *Turned Out By My Husband's Best Friend* had me looking at her ass like she was crazy; yet, I enjoyed the book.

"Uggh! I ain't feeling this word count shit," Tyanna stated as she ambled down the stairs with her laptop and notebook in hand.

"Well, I suggest you get your ass at the table with the rest of them and start feeling that shit," I spat with a smile on my face. My normal way of encouraging her to make shit happen, which always ended with her sitting at the damn table beating the keys up with a smile on her face.

"First of all, C, I ain't feelin' this shit right now. Anyways, why you tellin' me what to do, yo' ass need to be on the phone with Polo. I got so tired of him interrupting Ponytail and my conversation. Call that damn man, and when you do … I will sit at that damn table and bust those keys down."

"I am not about to argue with you about that damn ultimatum you just tried to give me," I laughed as my fucking phone dinged again.

"Got damn, Dorsey, respond to that nigga!" Sunny yelled, calling me by my last name.

"What have you not wanting to talk to him?" Tyanna asked as I muted my phone.

I didn't tell my girls that Polo and I had partially slept together. Hell, I didn't tell them that he came over to the house.

"I just don't. I like not having my mind wondering and pondering," I told her as my phone lit up.

"You slept with him didn't you?" she asked.

"She busted that four yeard of non-dick getting pussy open!" Ke'Lena and Vanice yelled in unison as their asses walked into the living room.

Laughter filled my home before they asked me thousands of questions, which I didn't answer any.

"Oh bitch, you gonna leak the press and when you do I … am … all … for … it," Ke'Lena stated as she clapped her hands towards the end of her statement before waltzing towards the kitchen table with her laptop and notebook.

Shortly afterwards, Tyanna was sitting at the table amongst the other writers. As Vanice took a seat beside me, I laid back and thought about the day I met Tyanna, Ke'Lena, and Vanice.

Our freshman year of high school, they were new to the city. We had Algebra and Biology classes together. The new student trio easily talked amongst themselves because they had one thing in common. I saw that we could benefit the fuck out of each other. Vanice and Ke'Lena were horrible in that damn math class; thus, the teacher asked for me to tutor them. I was horrible in Biology; thus, Tyanna, Vanice, and Ke'Lena came to my rescue. Within that first week of school, I introduced them to Crystal, and it was on and popping.

Ding. Dong. Ding. Dong. Ding. Dong.

"Now, who can fuck in this kind of weather?" Sunny stated in an agitated manner, causing Vanice and me to bust out laughing.

Whenever someone does some repetitive shit like calling or ringing the doorbell back to back, Sunny's ass get agitated quickly.

As I hopped away from the sofa, I said while laughing, "I could … if I was fucking."

"Who is it?" I asked the closer I approached my door.

Silence.

"I said who is it?" I inquired again as I pressed my nose to the expensive front door.

As I peeped through the peephole, my breath was taken away as Ke'Lena yelled, "Well, bitch who at the door?"

Trying to get my game face on, I ignored my friend as I opened the door.

"Um, yeah?" I replied casually as I glared at Polo's sexy ass wearing a pair of black gym shorts, a white muscle shirt, black socks, and a pair of male thot Nike sliders.

Not saying a word to me, Polo aggressively rushed my ass against the wall as he shoved his mouth onto mine — parting my lips with his tongue. Grabbing me by my waists, an excited gasp left my mouth and rushed into his as we tongued each other down.

My body was on cloud nine as my mind was on cloud zero. There was no way in hell I was going to let my body take over my mind. I was not about to let Polo swoop me like he did the other bitches by the usage of his wonderfully skilled sex abilities.

"Ooou, shit! Shit is about to get spicy in this motherfucka tonight!" Crystal yelled before the others piped in.

"Yassssss, bitch, yassss!"

"I want to redo that night. I badly fucked up. May I?" Polo growled as he made sure that my pussy was sitting on top of that long, fat dick of his.

Before I had the chance to say anything, those damn no manners having, down to ride bitches of mine chanted, "Let him! Let him! Let him, smassshhhh!"

"Mane, I swear y'all are wild as fuck." Polo stated as I tried to shove his arms off me while trying to get out of his embrace.

"Nawl, Cella, I'm not lettin' you get down. I'm goin' to carry you to the room I left you standin' feelin' some type of way in."

"And that is the reason why you are going to put me down. I'm not feeling you like that Polo. You cool and all, but I'm good love. It's time for you to go," I told him with as much authority as I could muster.

"I just know this bitch didn't sit up here and lie like she don't want that man," Vanice stated.

Growling as he closed the door, Polo sternly yet sexily said, "I was hopin' that I didn't have to man handle yo' ass."

CHAPTER THIRTEEN
Polo

"What you gonna do, Polo?" Crystal laughed, distracting Cella like I hoped she would.

In a flash I had her ass in the corner of the wall besides the door with my fingers strategically surfing through her drenching pussy.

"That is my cue to get the fuck on with this word count challenge," Sunny stated quickly before continuing, "Um, ladies, that means y'all asses as well. Vanice, get yo' ass at the table and come test read something for me."

"I ain't gon' keep apologizin' an' you givin' me yo' ass to kiss. I ain't gon' keep blowin' up yo' damn phone an' you won't respond. I ain't gon' keep doin' that shit before I lose my fuckin' mind an' apply pressure to yo' ass," I spoke through clenched teeth as my index and middle fingers tapped on Cella's G-spot, causing her ass to stand on her tiptoes and moan.

"I keep tellin' yo' ass that I'm sorry, an' you brush a nigga away like I'm a motherfuckin' bug or somethin'. I don't like that shit. Do you hear what the fuck I'm sayin' to you, Cella?" I asked as I quickened the pace of how I served my fingers into the pussy I couldn't wait to put my mouth on.

With her mouth hanging open, showing a nigga those dazzling eight gold teeth in her mouth, Cella's eyes rolled in the back of her head. Chuckling, I applied more pressure to her pussy as my mouth gently clamped on her left nipple.

"Fuckkkk!" she passionately screamed while her legs shook as her sticky juices flooded onto my fingers.

"Dammnnnn!" her girls stated loudly.

"You can sleep over, boy, it's cool," Cella whined as she placed her loving, lustful eyes on me.

"Oh, word?" I chuckled while removing my fingers from her pussy.

As she nodded her head, I nodded mine while moving my wet fingers to my mouth.

As she wagged her finger at me, Cella snatched my pussy juice soaked fingers to her mouth, she cooed, "I love tasting me, too."

That damn woman sloppily yet beautifully sucked my fingers, all the while staring in my damn eyes. I lost my soul as she gave my fingers the best suck and lick of their lives.

"Got daaammmnnn, it, nih!" I loudly growled as I rushed her ass to her bedroom.

Once inside, we didn't waste any time. I stripped Cella out of her clothes as she eagerly got me out of mine. Instead of getting on the bed, that woman dropped to her knees and toyed with my dick and balls.

"I prefer to go first, woman," I stated in a boss tone.

"I ain't here fo' no conversation. I ain't really tryin' to talk. Can a bitch be honest, baby? I just came here to fuck," Cella voiced in that bossy yet sweet ass timbre that I loved.

With a sneaky smile on her face, she reached for a small black remote control. Within a short amount of time, Post Malone featuring Jeremih song "Fuck" blasted through the speakers of her nice black and chrome stereo system.

Ah so this is the song that had me intrigued wit' her ass, I thought as I glared at her.

Cella placed her warm, wet mouth on the head of my dick. In seconds, she had me gone. That damn woman took her time sucking, licking, and kneading my balls all the while humming all with the artists on the song. My head flopped back so hard I just knew my motherfucking neck was on the verge of breaking.

"Shiitt, Cella," I groaned as I weakly placed my hand on the part of her head that was shaved low with six tatted stars on it.

Three songs played as she gave my dick the best talk it ever had. I had been close to climaxing but I prayed to the Lord not to let me be a wimp and crash out. My man was strong and deep in her mouth as I assumed that she was on a mission to make me hers.

Young Bleu's "Wanna Fuck" song came on, and that woman showed me what it really was like to fuck with her.

"Show this pussy just how sorry you are for disappointing her," she voiced through clenched teeth while taking a seat on the bed, followed by playing in the very hole I was going to be in all night.

"Say no mo'."

Like she told me to show, I did that and so much more. I had her back arched from the time I blew on that pretty pussy of hers until she was begging for me to get up and enter her—thirty motherfucking minutes later. I had to make sure that I had Cella gone off my head game just as much as she had me gone off her.

"Shitt! Polooo!" she loudly whimpered as I brought her to another gut wrenching, beautiful orgasm.

Seeing the tears drip down her face for the tenth time, I decided that it was time for her to show me how well she could ride the dick that was about to change her whole fucking life!

"Ride this dick. Let a nigga know how bad you want him inside of you," I growled as I snatched her ass off her back, placing her on top of me.

She tried reaching for the nightstand with all the condoms in, and I nipped that shit in the bud. As she looked at me as if I lost my mind, some crazy ass song came on talking about riding a stick. I didn't know what in the fuck got into Cella, but that damn woman got up on my dick and showed the fuck out—on the inches that she could muster inside of her.

"My damn," I spat as I saw her competitive ass twerking on at least seven inches of my man.

I really felt like the nigga on the song was coaching her ass because Cella rode the fuck out of my tool. My tender dick ass didn't have a dog in the fight I called myself bringing to her. I had to say that she slaughtered my ass by the time she dropped low—titties all in a nigga's chest—and made that pussy do some type of tornado motion. Milawd! I was done! My nut was ready to deep in that pussy—running wildly.

Jonesin' For A Boss Chick: A Montgomery Love Story

As the nigga on the radio said several times to sit on it, Cella's ass did that all the while slowly popping that pussy of hers. Her legs started shaking and I knew she was close to the finish line. With a hard dick, even after I nutted, I flipped the tables and ironed that pussy out just the way I needed and wanted to!

"Poloo!" she hollered as she began pulling her hair.

"What?" I questioned as I slowed my pace and made love to the one person I never wanted to disrespect.

Bringing my head closer to hers, she whispered in my ear. When she was done speaking, I looked at her with so much passion and admiration until I understood why she waited so long to even let a nigga be in her presence if he wasn't paying for a tattoo or car repairs.

The shit Lil' Momma whispered in my ear had me giving her something that I knew she never had and that I never gave any other female—all of me!

***

Sunday, June 10th, 2018

I woke to Marvin Sapp's song "The Best in Me" playing at a nice decibel as the aroma of breakfast lingered throughout Cella's bedroom. Rising from the comfortable bed, I stretched as

I thought about the beautiful woman that was missing from bed.

"He's mine, I'm his," Cella sang as she stepped into the room, wearing a lovely fitted, coral pantsuit, complimentary business appeasing pearl jewelry.

Her voice and Marvin Sapp's song was heaven sent. I loved the song, but Cella made me fall more in love with it as she continued singing the gospel song.

"Good morning, beautiful," I told her as I smiled.

"Good morning," she spoke before winking at me.

"Ah, someone getting ready for church, huh?"

Nodding her head, she replied, "You should be too. We are leaving in an hour. Your plate is in the microwave. I asked VJ to stop by your crib to grab you some church attire. I hope you don't mind."

With a smile on my face as I strolled towards her, I voiced, "No, I don't mind at all, but um I have to be at my parents' church."

"I know. Your parents told me about your father's anniversary, yesterday. They invited my ladies and me. Thus, we are up and ready. The fellas are downstairs eating. So, I suggest you get your behind in the tub now."

"Yes, ma'am," I announced as I pulled her into my arms.

There was no need for us to speak to each other as we glared into each other's eyes. The tight, loving embrace and the look in our eyes were enough to speak for a million years to come.

"Never would have made it!" Ke'Lena sang beautifully from afar.

"Whoa, she can blow," I spat in amazement at the voice that Ke'Lena had on her.

Chuckling, Cella replied, "You think she can blow ... wait for it ... Sunny will be chiming in shortly."

I be damned if she didn't, and I was amazed at the ladies that I didn't know had singing abilities that sent chills through your body.

"You need to take a shower. Hurry up," Cella voiced in a bossy timbre before continuing, "I will have your clothes laid on the bed."

Nodding my head, I dashed into the bathroom. I was blown at the ladies that I had the pleasure of being around for close to a month. Every day they surprised me. They were truly gifted women; granted, they were freaky as all out doors but they were the truth!

Once I showered, I dressed and skipped down the spiral staircase. I was granted by my fam and the ladies dressed in their church attire with huge smiles on their faces. It was as if they had done a complete three-sixty. Not a soul said a curse word, not a soul was being mannerless—especially Ke'Lena and Vanice. They were on chill mode. That was very unusual for them.

Waltzing into the kitchen, a breakfast plate and a glass of orange juice were sitting on the table. Cella was wiping down the kitchen counters as she ordered for me to eat. I saluted her causing her to chuckle as she looked at me before winking her eye. While I ate, images of me saying my final goodbyes to my children began taking a toll on me. I had to drop my head and began to pray—something that I hadn't done in a long time.

I asked God for a simple favor—to give me the strength to deal with not being able to see my sons in the flesh. Afterwards, I felt as if something overcame me. I didn't feel completely better about the situation; yet, I didn't feel like I did when I first learned that I was sons-less.

"It's time to go," Cella stated the moment I finished eating.

"What cars are we getting in?" Crystal asked as she strolled towards a small door in the back of the living room.

"Um, we are getting into the Excursion," Cella softly breathed before continuing, "Polo, I don't know the way to your parents' church."

As she handed me the keys to another of her vehicles, we exited her sweet-smelling, cleaned home. Along the way to my parents' church, I felt at ease. I had a strong team standing behind me, and a nigga was extra thankful for that. Halfway to my parents' neck of the woods, my cell phone rang.

Detaching it from the holster, I saw my mother's name displaying across the screen.

"Hello, Momma."

"Hey, Son. How are you this morning?" she asked sweetly as I heard older ladies in the background talking.

"I'm okay. How about you?"

"The Lord allowed me to wake up this morning with good health, so I will not complain," she stated softly before continuing, "Son, yesterday was a very hard day for you and I will completely understand if you aren't able to come to church for your father's anniversary."

"Momma, I'm actually okay enough to attend church this morning. Shoot, I didn't have a dog in that fight if I wanted to.

You invited some exceptional ladies to Dad's pastor anniversary that would not let me sit still if I wanted to."

With an excited tone, my mother said, "Oou, are you talking Cella, Vanice, Crystal, Ke'Lena, Sunny, Shanice, and Tyanna?"

"Yes."

"Son, I don't know where you and your crazy cousins have met those women at, but I know one darn thing … y'all need to keep them on y'all's team. I'm impressed with the way they took over the kitchen yesterday and helped out. It seemed as if they were a part of the family. Never had I seen your daughters take to women, especially Cella, the way that they did."

With a curious look on my face, I briefly looked at Cella while asking my mother, "Momma, will you explain the last part, please?"

"Jalia had a woman visitor yesterday," my mother stated slowly.

Instantly, I was thrown off. Thus, I asked, "Um, who came to see my daughter yesterday? What did she want?"

Immediately, Cella and her ladies on top of my mother burst out laughing.

"Son, Jalia had her first encounter with a period," my mother chuckled as the women laughed at me.

"Oh. Oooh. Um, um," I stated as my mother continued.

"Cella helped her understand what was going on. That's why Cella, your sisters, and your daughters left for a store run. I think the girls really like Cella."

I do too. I'm just hopin' I don't do anything stupid again an' push her away.

"Son, I like Cella. If you are not feeling a future with her then I suggest you let the next man claim that wonderful, heart filled with love woman. No need in toying with her mind. I highly believe it was toyed enough. Now, I will see y'all once y'all get here," she stated quickly as I heard Sister Morris calling my mother's name.

Ending the phone with 'I love you's', I had a smile on my face as I looked at the beautiful, bossy angel sitting in the passenger seat.

"Thank you fo' helpin' Jalia out yesterday," I voiced as I connected Cella's and my hands.

"Aww, that is so sweet!" our crew yelled happily.

"No problem," she replied.

"Y'all are just too cute together," the ladies cooed as the fellas agreed.

I think so also.

"Y'all get on my nerves but a sister love y'all to the moon and back," Cella voiced sweetly as I kissed the back of her hand.

God, I have one mo' prayer request. That you allow Cella an' I grow into somethin' beautiful, somethin' so special an' precious.

CHAPTER FOURTEEN
Cella

Sunday, June 10th

   I was ecstatic to see my little one dressed in a beautiful dress that she had to have. The little white kitten heels that she stepped in had me thinking about putting her into modeling. Her thick, three differently naturally colored coiled hair was mixed into the box braids that I paid the Africans to braid yesterday.

   I wasn't surprised to see some of our church home family members in attendance for the normal services at Freemont Baptist Episcopal Church. My parents were church going people; thus, I knew they had heard about Pastor Willis' pastor anniversary. As the service went about in a heartfelt and loving manner, I had to wipe my eyes and Polo's several times. The spirit overcame me as I looked at my loving family and friends. There wasn't anything else that I could be more thankful for. The message that Pastor Willis delivered I knew he had his son in mind.

   By the time the pastor anniversary ceremony started, I felt the need to sing. Thus, I secretly approached Polo's parents and asked them was there a way that I could squeeze into the program. The smile that spread across their faces informed me that I would be making a special appearance on the stage.

"Sure. What song would you like to sing?" Pastor Willis asked.

"One that I know everyone in here can relate too, especially Polo ... Yolanda Adam's *Open My Heart*."

"Oh, my," Polo's mother stated before she placed her hands over her mouth, elated.

"By all means, I would love for you to open the ceremony with that lovely song, dear," his father stated with a huge grin on his face.

"She's the one for him, Joe. She's the one for our son," his mother stated as tears filled her eyes.

This is starting to get a little weird for me.

They pulled me into a tight embrace. Shortly afterwards, they sent me to an area where the choir was practicing. They introduced me to the choir director before leaving. He asked me did I want to practice the song I wanted to sing, and I told him no.

Ten minutes later, I had a standing ovation from my parents, my ladies, and my daughter. A sight that brought tears to my face was the sight of seeing my brother standing beside Xyla — holding her hand.

Like always, my sudden urge to sing and boom there is my brother. A non-church goer.

The choir director introduced me to the church goers. Once he winked at me, I knew it was my time to make tears stream down people's faces.

"Alone in a room, it's just me and you," my soft sweet voice sang as I looked around the large room.

I completely relaxed and let God use me as his vessel. Like I told Polo's parents, I knew there would be someone that needed to hear my voice sing Yolanda Adam's song. I was so into the song that I didn't know that I left the choir section, standing in front of Polo singing and gently rubbing his face. He broke down, and I backed away as I nodded my head at VJ. Instantly, he and the other fellas had my Polo's back as I sang the song, focusing on the other half of the church members.

As the song came to a closure, I had the entire church wiping their faces as they stood giving me a standing ovation. Polo's wet eyes were on me as my moist eyes never left his face. I winked my eyes at him before I strolled towards the choir director whom was wiping his face.

"You did a wonderful job. God used you beautifully today, Cella. May he continue to bless you," he stated as I gave him the microphone back.

"Thank you," I stated before walking towards the seating area with my family.

The ceremony kicked off and might I say it was beautiful and the message delivered was what everyone, including my daughter, needed to hear. Towards the end of the ceremony, Polo's mother and several of the deaconesses approached me about ending the ceremony with another song of my choice. As I gave thought, the rarest thing happened to me in all of the years I have attended any church; the church goers loudly asked for another song by me.

"Do it, beautiful," Polo whispered in my ear as he squeezed my hand.

With a smile on my face, I looked at Sunny and Ke'Lena. I bucked my eyes at them, and they shot up like a rocket.

Standing, I looked at the lovely ladies of Freemont Baptist Episcopal Church and told them softly, "I would like to have Sunny and Ke'Lena sing along with me."

"Y'all are going to have this church in an uproar," my brother stated with a smile on his face.

"That's the plan."

"Go handle that, sis," he replied before blowing me a kiss.

Before I took a step, I looked at Ke'Lena and Sunny before saying, "I will kick it off. I'm going to projectile our favorite song by the time I reach the end of the pew."

"Okay," they replied in unison.

"Never would have made it!" I yelled beautifully.

The church went crazy. Before I passed the pew, my parents were sitting on, Xyla was beautifully and loudly executing the song—in such a manner that brought joy to me and everyone in the medium-sized sanctuary. My baby was blowing, sounding like a grown woman.

Oh my, listen to my baby, I thought as I extended my hand for her to place her little hand in.

"I'm stronger, I'm wiser," we sang as the church folks stood, sang, and swayed their bodies as their hands were in the air.

God placed his high beams on us as the visiting pastors and Pastor Willis shook hands. As the song ended, my ladies and I looked at each as we welcomed the feeling of being used in the right way. We welcome the gift that God allowed us to have and share with those in front of us. Most importantly, we welcomed being a child of God. There was no better feeling than the one we had as we waltzed down the aisles.

Once the ceremony was over, we dined in the fellowship hall. Praises and blessings were being shared amongst everyone. The food, conversation, and aura were great. My parents couldn't stop raining kisses on Xyla's and my head. After we finished eating, we waltzed into the front of the church. I was stopped by the choir director. He hugged and thanked me once more for a beautiful performance before he thanked Xyla, Ke'Lena, and Sunny.

As I walked my daughter to my parents' vehicle, my ladies and the fellas, minus Polo, were heading to my SUV.

"Princess Xyla," Polo stated sweetly from behind us.

"Sir?" my daughter said as she looked at Polo, blushing.

As he introduced himself, she was smiling.

"Maybe one day, you, your mom, myself, and daughters could hang out? If you would like that."

"I would love that, but everything is up to Boss Mommy," she grinned.

Chuckling, I replied, "I think Boss Mommy would love that also."

We chatted a little while longer before my brother popped into our circle. I introduced Polo to my family. They shook hands. Of course, my brother—being my brother—gave Polo sweet church words.

"She's my favorite sister. So, you know what that means right?" Joshua stated seriously yet in a polite manner.

"I do," Polo stated seriously.

"Well, nice to meet you. At least I know she won't be a spinster for the rest of her life," he joked as they dapped each other up.

"Boy, go on somewhere," my mother chuckled before hugging us.

"Cella, will you be able to make the annual family vacation tomorrow?" my father asked me.

"Yes. The shop will be closed for a week. Oh, and the ladies are coming too."

"*Duh*. Do you really have to say that every year, Cella?" Joshua stated smartly.

"Tell us something that we don't know already, Cella," my parents joked.

As I blew them air kisses before saying that I loved them, Polo's name was loudly called by a voice that I recognized.

"Ugh," he stated as my parents slipped into my father's truck.

"Unwanted female, huh?" I asked as he connected our hands, pulling me towards my truck.

"Yep."

"Well, you should know not to sex them all the same." I shot back as I looked at him with a crazy facial expression.

"See, what had happened was." He snickered, causing me to laugh.

The moment we arrived at my truck, the chick was right behind us calling Polo's name.

"Oh, so *this* is why you won't return a call or text? Is *this* the reason why you are treating me like I'm nothing? Is *this* the reason why you acting like we didn't have anything special?" she inquired, ensuring to put emphasis on the word this as she looked at me.

Not willing to let the devil get me out of my good mood, I looked at Polo and sweetly said, "Handle *that* so we can go to my place."

"Nothin' to handle, beautiful. Joana knows she's old news. She been in church all this time. Trust she knows what it is between you an' me," he stated sternly while looking at me as he walked backward towards the passenger door.

Once he opened the door, he sexily growled, "Your chariot awaits you, beautiful. Hop in."

Before I could walk amble my pretty, self-made behind into my vehicle, the bitch had the nerves to grab my arm. Immediately, my girls and I forgot that we were on church grounds. We weren't loud; yet, we had some non-church words running out of our mouths.

"Aye, y'all get in this damn truck," Gwap stated in a low tone as people began looking our way.

Knowing when to be disrespectful, we bit down on our attitude as one-by-one we filed into my truck. I was the last to get in, and that broad was glaring at me with pure hatred in her eyes.

Sinisterly chuckling, I spat, "Bitches like you love coming for me, but don't have a degree in certified ass beating with a concentration in ignorance to fuck with a strand on my head."

"He'll be back to me like he always does just like he wa--," she stated before Polo yelled for me to get in.

Doing exactly what he said, I smiled sweetly as I winked my eye at the broad.

"I swear you be sayin' som' fly ass shit," VJ voiced before laughing.

"Because I'm a fly, boss chick," I told him as Polo pulled away from the frowning broad.

Along the way to my house, Polo received a phone call from his daughters. The look on that man's face was priceless as he chatted with his girls. Now, that was the type of man that I wished I had a child with. Instead of the asshole that helped me create my beautiful princess.

Clearing his throat, Polo piped into the phone, "Um, I am not comfortable talkin' to y'all 'bout that. Where y'all Mommas at?"

"Go figures. Well, um, hold on she right here," he stated into the phone as my cell phone rang.

As I grabbed my phone and saw LaJuan's name, I rolled my eyes as I placed Polo's phone to my ear followed by saying, "Hello, ladies."

"Hey, Cella," they replied in unison.

In a flash, Jalia asked, "So, I was wondering what I do about these cramps and what is best for clothing since I feel uncomfortable?"

"Um, I don't want to step on your mother toes or anything. I think you should ask her for help first, Jalia."

"I did, and she told me to read about periods and stuff."

What the fuck?

As I told her what she needed to do, I was fuming at what type of mother would leave their child to the Internet when her ass could tell her daughter what she needed to know. While I was on the phone with Polo's daughters, my phone was ringing off the hook. Soon as the call ended between the sweet girls and me, I retrieved my phone. Dialing LaJuan's number, I was ready to give his ass the business.

"Why in the fuck are you calling my phone like that, LaJuan?" I asked angrily as the voices in my SUV ceased.

"Um, I need your help," his sorry ass stated.

"Nigga, you don't need my help with shit. When in the fuck have you ever helped me? Oh yeah, you did when you gave me Xyla."

"Cella, chill. I need you to come bail me out."

Laughing, I said, "What in the fuck do you mean come bail you out? Why you ain't calling your fucked-up hip momma dude?"

"Well, I be damn," my girls said as the guys said 'oh shit'.

"Come on, Cella. Don't be that way."

"Dude, get the fuck off--," I stated before he cut me off.

"Mane, look my bail is five-hundred dollars. You can go to a bond's man and pay fifty dollars. I will give you the money back. The nice officer let me call you several times before sending me to the back," he stated in a desperate manner.

I had to laugh at the nigga on my phone. The audacity that nigga had to call me for help was unbelievable. This was the same dude that didn't call our child on her birthday. The same motherfucker that acted as if Xyla wasn't nothing to him. The same dude that had a bitch approach me about a damn lie that he concocted.

If I wasn't Marcella Nicole Dorsey, then I didn't know who the fuck I was. I laid that bastard out so bad that I knew I was going to hell for the way I cursed him out and made him feel like the shit he truly was.

"Now, bitch don't you ever call my motherfucking phone again or you will see me. Call your bald-headed ass momma not me! Call that crooked tooth bitch that approached me at The Shack not me!"

"Not the baldheaded ass momma!" The Willis crew yelled out before laughing.

"Wit' her soggy titty ass," Ke'Lena spat loudly, causing everyone to laugh.

As Polo pulled into my driveway, I was woosah'ing like a motherfucker. Just that damn quick Satan had to bring his small dick ass in my nice aura and fuck it up.

"In other news, where is y'all's family trip takin' place?" Polo inquired, changing the mood.

"Nashville, Tennessee," I told him as I resume to my normal self.

"Fellas, you think we can afford to take a week off?" he asked with a sneaky smile on his face.

"Not really but what the hell ... we only live once right?" Russ said.

"We gotta do a trip with the kids. My baby momma on my ass about getting' the bo--," Big stated before cutting his statement short.

An eerie silence overcame us before Polo looked at Big and said, "Never again will you cut off yo' sentence 'bout yo' boys. True, mine are not here. But don't ever feel the need to not discuss them in fear of how I may feel. Understood?"

"Roger that," Big stated before telling Polo that he loved him.

As we filed out of my truck, I learned things about the guys that I never knew. All of their asses were die hard parents, but their children didn't live in a fifty-mile radius of Montgomery, and some of their baby mothers were coo-coo.

"So, when exactly are we making arrangements to get our churren?" Ponytail asked.

"By the middle of July," I replied.

"Bet," Ponytail responded.

Clearing his throat, Gwap questioned, "Yo' folks won't mind us bargin' into y'all's family vacation?"

"Not at all. Just don't smell like weed or curse and y'all will be good in their eyes," I told them as we exited my truck.

The moment we arrived inside of my cool home, the fuckery began. My crew was back to their usual selves as Vanice put on some trap music.

"Um, so when are we going to y'all's crib?" Big asked my ladies.

They spat in unison, "Our cribs ain't big enough for all of us. Why in the hell do you think we at Cella's? She was the smarter one and decided to get a huge crib and shit. She like doing all that cleaning and dusting."

As Tyanna and Crystal strolled into the kitchen, I called my parents and let them know that we have more guests joining us on our family vacation. Of course, they were excited. After the call ended, I told the fellas that our vacation was a go. Afterwards, we began discussing the trip we were going to take with our children. Everyone agreed on Disney World; however, we couldn't agree on dates. Therefore, we said that we would make the decision soon as we could.

"Um, Cella, may I talk to you in yo' room please?" Polo asked seductively before licking his oh so skillful lips, the moment our crew began snuggling underneath one another.

With a raised eyebrow and a tingling clit, I sauntered my ass to my room with Polo sexily growling behind me.

As he closed the bedroom door, followed by locking it, he groaned, "Will you allow me to show you how thankful I am fo' you bein' in a nigga's presence?"

"Yes," I lovingly cooed as I pulled him towards me.

"Good. Now, get yo' ass on that bed 'cause I got a lot of showin' to do."

CHAPTER FIFTEEN
Polo

Tuesday, June 12th

Nashville, Tennessee was the place to be. It was refreshing for me to be in a different setting, hanging around genuine people. Joshua, Mr. Dorsey, my crew, and I got along a lot better than I thought we would. Believe it or not, Mr. Dorsey and I hit it off more than me and her brother. For hours, Mr. Dorsey and I talked about old school cars, sports, investing money into stocks and bonds, his time in the military. He was a veteran with plenty of money — thanks to him doing right with his money. I learned a thing or two about stocks and bonds, which had me curious to look into a couple.

Joshua wasn't into the old school cars, but he was certainly into sports and dog fighting. Of course, Joshua and I put up a nice bet for the Alabama and Auburn football game. Joshua was like the old me but more sneaky with it. He sold drugs while his main occupation was being a truck driver. Like his father, Joshua also invested in stocks and bonds.

Cella's mother was just as sweet, loving, and caring as her daughter. I saw why Cella shined like a diamond. She had parents that would cross hell and back for her. That adored her as much as they adored their son. Mrs. Dorsey was a real housewife, who's never worked outside of her home a day in her life. She was truly dedicated to her husband and children. She met Mr. Dorsey when they were fifteen years old and gotten married when they were seventeen.

I knew Cella and Joshua had a sister, but she was not amongst us. Every time I asked Cella about her sibling, she would say that her sister was a wild one that she didn't particularly care for at the moment. The tone she spoke in concerning her sister was enough for me to leave the things alone. Even Cella's parents and brother didn't bring up the mysterious sister that they mentioned from time to time. I knew then that it was more to the story with the sister that was mentioned but never present—especially for her niece's birthday party.

The most obnoxious, loud mouth familiar voiced skeezer and another familiar voice spat in unison, "Hello, is anyone here?"

What the fuck? Lord, please don't let this be, I thought as my line of vision was placed on two bitches that I had threesomes with from time to time, stood at the balcony of the Dorsey's large cabin home.

"My, my, my. Isn't this going to be a lovely weekend?" Traneice stated as Joana looked at me with angry eyes.

"Now, who can fuck in this kind of weather?" Sunny stated as her and the ladies stepped onto the back steps.

"I sho' wanna know," Ponytail said as I thanked God that Cella's parents were gone out on an adventure of their own.

"So, what brings you to this neck of the woods, Polo?" Traneice asked, running her tongue across her teeth.

"I brought him to our neck of the woods, little sister," Cella said sweetly as she climbed the steps with a hunting rifle strapped to her left shoulder.

The fellas cleared their throats as they said, "*Little sister.*"

Oh, shit.

"Oou, sissy, you must've known I was feenin' fo' som' mo' of Polo Willis," Traneice stated in a seductive manner.

With a crazy facial expression, Cella oddly said, "Now, who can really fuck in this kind of weather for real?"

"Traneice, remember I was telling you about a female that was at Polo's church with him?" Joana said as I saw Cella and her girls getting ready to show out.

"Yep."

"Well, your sister is the one I saw him with ... holding hands," Joana stated in a matter-of-fact timbre.

Chuckling, Traneice asked, "Cella, that nigga got a long, fat ass dick, don't he?"

Oh, shit. Oh, shit, was all that I could think about before shit was about to hit the fan—all of it!

CHAPTER SIXTEEN
Cella

"Now, wait a whole fuckin' minute," Joshua stated as he waltzed onto the back patio.

"Explain," I told my trifling ass sister.

"Let's just say that Polo isn't a stranger to Joana an' me ... threesome style ... sometimes one on one. Whichever Joana an' I prefer," she replied in a tone that set my fucking soul on fire and fueled my heart with hatred for her.

"Oh, wow," my besties sang.

"How long y'all been kicking it, Traneice?" I tried asking calmly.

"Three years an' countin'," she replied with a smile that had me boiling.

"Mmm, and counting, huh?" I voiced as I began clicking my nails together.

"Real recent too," Joana stated before laughing.

"Cella, we need to talk now," Polo stated while looking at me.

Ignoring him, I placed my eyes on the bitch that had the audacity to step to me on church grounds and asked, "Just how recent?"

"Thirteen days ago to be exact ... what a lovely late Tuesday night until early in the morning fun we had," Traneice spoke as if she was reminiscing on the night her encounter with Polo took place.

Instantly clearing my throat, I felt dizzy as I knew I had to escape the environment I was placed in—unexpectedly.

"Oh wow. Um, I need to ... I need to go," I heard myself saying in a confused manner before I walked into the cabin as my ladies were behind me.

"You thought you had a husband in the makin', huh, Cella?" Traneice asked nastily as she turned and faced the inside of the beautifully decorated wooden style, dark-brown cabin.

"That's enough, Traneice!" Joshua yelled, angrily.

Continuing, she said, "Sorry big sis. You know you have bad choice in niggas, yet they do be fine as fuck. They only want you because you have money an' got a tight ass body. You will never find you a good man, sweetheart."

I had enough of that bitch's mouth. It was time for me to finally put my hands on the one bitch that had it out for me since I could remember. She was going to get the ass whooping my parents and brother's saved her from. She wanted me to be one of those bitches in the streets; then, got damn it I had to give it to her as if she was just a regular bitch in the streets.

No one could hold or stop me as I knocked Joana out as Traneice wildly swung like a mad woman. Grabbing her ass by the puny wrists attached to her body, I brought my knee to my sister's stomach with such force that the hateful bitch couldn't howl out from the pain. The moment she lost her pathetic will to fight, I gave her ass something to think about. I badly wished that I would blank out and kill her ass; yet, I guess that wasn't God's plan.

Seeing that she was defeated, I dragged the bitch to the corner of the porch where there was a lone chair. As I evilly and nastily glared at my twenty-eight year old sister, I shook my head.

"No more warnings. Every time I see you and you look at me wrong, I'mma tear off in your ass," I told her in an unsteady breathing tone.

As I walked away from Traneice, my eyes never left her. Standing int the middle of the porch, I blankly stated, "Polo, let's go hunting."

"Um, Cella, I think--," my brother stated before I cut him off.

"Joshua, you know me. So, shut the fuck up!" I yelled before placing my eyes on Polo and speaking my fucking demand.

"Will y'all talk some sense into her?" Joshua asked my girls as I waltzed inside of the cabin to retrieve another assault rifle.

"My name is Bennett an' I ain't in it," Ke'Lena voiced seriously as she took a seat.

The porch was quiet as I threw the rifle to Polo.

"Move som'," I spoke through clenched teeth as I descended the steps.

If I had've stayed on that porch with my sister one minute longer, I knew that I was going to do some serious harm to her. Shooting was my way of calming down. All types of thoughts crossed my mind as I wanted to hit Polo in the face with the butt of the rifle.

As we quickly stepped away from my parents' cabin, the eerie silence must've gotten to him.

"Cella, I didn't know that Traneice was your sister. She always said that she was the only child. Not that I asked anything personal. That night I left your home, I didn't want to physically hurt you. I needed rough nasty sex, and I didn't want you feeling as if you were just a piece of ass to me. I wanted to take my frustration out on someone's daughter ... just you," he voiced sincerely as what he said went in one ear and out of the other as a family of rabbits came into my line of vision.

I didn't give a damn about him fucking Traneice. I didn't give a single damn of him smashing my sister like the slut that she really was. That shit didn't faze me at all. What got the best of me was the fact that he left my home to seek the company of nothing bitches. He left me feeling busted and disgusted—that's what hurt me the most.

Quickly, I aimed the rifle at the rabbits and squeezed the trigger. Perfect kill after perfect kill was my motto when I hunted. Once I slaughtered the rabbits, I continued moving through the beautiful, serene woods. In the mood to let my behavior speak for me, I landed my eyes on birds sitting high in a tree at a nice distance.

"Cella, talk to me," Polo voiced as I aimed the gun towards the birds.

"Ple--," he stated as I pressed the trigger.

One by one those motherfucking birds fell to the ground.

Enough of killing animals psychopath, I thought as I placed the gun to my side.

Facing Polo, I nastily said, "Instead of talking to me that night … you chose to fuck with some nothing ass hoes. Now, you want me to talk to you. I find that shit real funny, Polo."

I walked off on his ass. While strolling behind me, Polo tried his best to get me to talk to him.

"They were just somethin' fo me to do. I haven't fucked wit' or called them since that night. I left that damn hotel like I always do … as if they ain't shit to me, which they aren't. I didn't do anything to them that I did to you, Cella."

Spinning around to face him, I ran my hand through my bone straight weave before saying, "Yes you did. You left them just like you left me as if I wasn't shit to you."

There was nothing left to be said; thus, I waltzed into the cabin with my head held high, my feelings tucked deep inside of my core, and a huge smile on my face—showcasing my pearly, white teeth and the permanent eight golds sitting pretty and blingy at the bottom, all the while concocting a master plan to make Joana and Traneice sweat.

The moment I planted my right foot on the first step, I looked at Polo and said, "I think we can get a lil' fucking in before my parents appear. Follow me to the room *we* will be staying in."

"Ahh, shit," Tyanna and Joshua spat while shaking their heads.

"Yep, just like that." I laughed as I sashayed my fine ass into the cabin with Polo on my heels.

***

Oh, the sweat I brought to Joana and Traneice's asses were exactly what I wanted to accomplish. They didn't like how Polo catered to me as I did the same for him. They couldn't stand that I sat on his lap, and he massaged every inch of my body, all the while gently yet sweetly placing kisses on the nape of my neck.

Oh, I was playing a lovely game with Polo as well. He didn't know that the moment we touched down in Alabama his ass was going to be history. Why not fuck and get all that I could out of him before I placed my pussy back under dick deprivation? Might as well get those four years of cobwebs knocked completely down before I let another set of cobwebs build.

"Y'all make such a lovely couple, Cella," my mother stated sweetly as she sat in my father's lap.

"You think so, Mommy? So, do I," I voiced in an innocent, young girl's voice — tormenting my sister and her company.

My girls coughed as I knew one of them lowly said bullshit — something that they did when I was being extremely petty.

"Traneice and Joana, why are you ladies so quiet?" my father asked while placing his brown peepers on them.

"No reason." They shot back as they sat in the corner of the living room—looking dumb as fuck.

"Traneice, what happened to your face honey?" my mother inquired shortly afterwards in a shocked tone.

Traneice didn't offer a word; however, I did. "I put my hands on her."

"What? Why?" my mother questioned as she stood to her feet.

"Honey, they are sisters and grown. They will have differences. Let them be," my father voiced softly as he pulled my mother onto his lap.

Placing my eyes on my sister, I patiently waited for her to answer our mother's question but she didn't. Rolling my eyes at the bitch that couldn't look at me, I wanted to tear off in her ass again. In the need to deter my mind, I stood all the while lightly chuckling.

Shortly afterwards, I happily said, "Mmm, dinner smells good. I think I will check on it."

"Something happened between the two of you, and I want to know what it was. So spill the beans," my mother announced with as much authority that she could muster before calling my brother's name.

"Momma, please don't put me in the middle of things," Joshua spoke as he was texting.

"Honey, let things be. They haven't killed each other in all these years, and they aren't now. Let them be," my father said as I slowly sashayed in between the seats my parents, sisters, and her minion of a friend.

With a smile on my face, I stopped beside my sister and bent towards her ear. With my lips close to her crusty ass ear, I messily and lowly whispered, "I enjoyed riding that big ass dick Polo got. I enjoyed him spreading my legs and tasting every ounce of the juices that flooded into his mouth from my low mileage pussy. I enjoyed sticking my tongue in his mouth and watch him sucking on it while he gently yet savagely finger fucked me. Oh, and I really enjoyed him sucking on all ten of my toes ... causing me to squeal his name. I think it's safe to say that he enjoyed me sucking the soul out of him as tears seeped down his face that he didn't want anyone but me. Rest assured little sister, when we touch down in Alabama you and that minion of yours can have him. He won't be of any use to me."

Standing erect, I loudly spat, "And I drop the mic."

"You think so? Well, how is this fo' a bomb? This is comin' from Joana *an'* me," she announced happily with a light chuckle as she threw two pregnancy tests at me.

"Oh, my," my girls and Polo's fam stated surprisingly — in unison.

With my game face on, I glared at my sister as if I didn't give a fuck. Why? Simple because I didn't give two fucks. My mind was settled the moment I decided that Polo and I were no longer going to entertain each other on that level. He's proven on more than one occasion that he wasn't what I needed in my daughter and my lives.

"Traneice and Cella, what in the world is going on?" our mother stated as Traneice stood, glaring at me.

"Now, I just dropped the mic, big sister." She laughed while glaring at me and rubbing her flat ass stomach, all the while pointing at Polo.

CHAPTER SEVENTEEN
Polo

Thursday, July 12th

"Hey, Shanice. Is Cella busy?" I asked as I held a bouquet of red, white, and pink fresh roses from my mother's flower bed.

"Hey, Polo. Um, she should be done shortly. You can have a seat if you like while I let her know you are here," she sweetly stated as she pushed her glasses up on her petite nose.

"Oh no. Don't tell her. I want to surprise her, that way she won't curve me from her work station," I told her quickly as I heard Cella's deep voiced client tell her that he loved the artwork.

Instantly, I became nervous at her reaction of me being at her business. Things hadn't been the same—fuck that—the moment Traneice stated that I was responsible for her and Joana's pregnancies, Cella and I were doomed. She didn't want to hear shit that I had to say. Instantly, there was uproar in the cabin as Cella laughed—hysterically before leaving with her girls and their luggage.

I texted and called her every day since then, and she refused to respond. I had to receive word from her ladies on her well-being, and boy I didn't like their response. Cella didn't show any negative emotions about what went down between the two of us. She didn't talk about me or none of that shit. Basically, she cut throat my ass out of her life. Whereas, I was a complete fucking mess. I couldn't eat, think, shit, or sleep peacefully knowing that Cella and I were not on the path that I had hoped we would be on. I was losing my mind thinking about what nigga she might have been entertaining.

"You are truly the damn best wit' yo' sexy self," a fuck nigga stated with much lust and adoration.

"Why, thank you, Nyko," Cella's soft voice spoke as the clinking of her heels sounded on the pretty black and gold marbled floor.

I knew that I had to get her to talk to me longer than five seconds; thus, I came up with a plan to get a tattoo—a large one. Quickly, I pulled out a wad of cash. Peeling off five-hundred dollars, I held the money out to Shanice.

With a raised eyebrow, she questioned, "Um. I would assume that you want a tattoo?"

"Yes," I replied as I felt my blood boiling.

"Would you like to pick out what you want?" she asked as my eyes zoned on Nyko's fuck ass and the most beautiful woman I'd ever seen.

"No. I want her to freestyle somethin' fo' me," I stated loudly as Cella stopped in her tracks as Nyko looked at me with eyes that I wished I could shoot out.

I know damn well she ain't tattooin' a fuckin' soul wit' that type of dress an' heels on. She ain't got on no damn pannies in that skin tight shit. I'm finna fuck her ass up!

"Polo Willis," Nyko breathed, causing my eyes to be taken off Cella.

"Nyko the Snake." I shot back with as much hatred I could muster.

Shaking his head as he chuckled in a disturbing manner, the fuck nigga that some women called a chocolate god placed his eyes on Cella.

"Same time next week?"

"Sure thing," she spoke as she bit on her bottom lip before fumbling with her hands, all the while looking at Nyko.

Immediately, I knew that I was going to nip some shit in the bud. There was no way she was going to link up with that nigga. He would suck her bank account dry before she would know it.

"If it ain't 'bout business my nigga ... stay the fuck away from Cella," I voiced sternly as I left the receptionist area.

"Who in the fuck are you to tell anyone to stay the fuck away from me. Hell, I told you to stay the fuck away, yet you won't do it," she voiced nastily and loudly while glaring at me.

As he blew a kiss to Cella, I had my hand on my gun with in a flash before Cella shouted, "Don't you fucking think about it Polo!"

"Pipe down, my nigga. You righteously ain't mad at me. You mad at the deceased bitch that robbed yo' ass blind while you were behind bars. The same bitch that snitched yo' ass out to be wit' me. I told her not to do that fuck shit, but hey, money hungry hoes do what they want. The same bitch that took those handsome, precious boys away from they dad ... to be wit' me. Once again, I told her ass not to do that triflin' ass shit, but hey, money hungry hoes do what they want. So, pipe down. I ain't do shit to you. Yo' deceased ass baby momma did that shit."

"Oh, my," Cella and Shanice spoke in unison.

Nyko and I stared each other down before he began walking towards the entrance/exit door as if he couldn't be touched. If it wasn't for me being in Cella's shop, I would've let several rounds off in that nigga's ass.

Placing his hand on the door, he turned around and looked me in the eyes. "On som' real shit, Polo, I didn't have any say so in what Janah did to you. After I learned of her stealin' yo' money an' dope, I knew that I couldn't have that bitch on my arms. She was not loyal or trustworthy, an' I couldn't have that type of negativity 'round me. I did treat yo' sons as if they were my own. I did fo' them when she wouldn't, which was often. She saw them as money an' a guaranteed way to not work. I saw them as a blessin' since I can't have kids of my own. Sorry fo' the loss of yo' boys, mane."

After his speech, I cleared my throat as I stood still glaring at him before he exited the shop. I had to give thought to what he said. Yet, that didn't stop me from not trusting that nigga. After all, a nigga would say anything to not have his head split the fuck open by that iron.

Putting my eyes on Cella, I said, "I want a special, beautiful tattoo wit' my kids' name. I don't care how you design it. I just want you to do it."

With teary eyes, she nodded her head followed by saying, "Sure thing. This one is on the house."

Strolling towards her with the bouquet of roses, I calmly announced, "I pay full price like everyone else. Understood?"

"You can't be in the doghouse and bossy too, Polo," she stated with a faint smile, trying to lighten the mood that lingered after Nyko exited her establishment with news that I didn't tell her.

Seriously yet gently, I replied, "How can I be in the doghouse when you have alienated yourself from me?"

"Well, we should get started on your tatt, huh?" she voiced oddly as she didn't look at me.

"Lead the way, beautiful."

As she did so, I had the urge to tell her the same shit I been texting and leaving on her voicemail for the past month—that I didn't get them hoes pregnant.

"Look Polo, what we had was cool and all, but you aren't what I need in a man. I'm sorry. We are done. We need to go back to the way we were before we incorporated sex and all that other shit. Let's just keep it at hey, bye, or when are you available to do tatts. Okay?" she hissed in a manner that would cause me to curse a broad out; yet, I found it cute when she did it.

"You sexy as fuck when you try to be mad an' hiss," I voiced as I shoved her against the door of her work station.

"Polo, either you want the tattoo or not?" she voiced harshly while rolling her eyes.

"I *need* the tattoo, you, an' Princess Xyla," I boldly stated as I scooped her ass up.

Shoving my tongue in her mouth, I made sure to slip my free hand between her thick thighs. Like I thought earlier, her ass didn't have on any panties. Horribly protesting for me to remove my hand, two fingers found the place I fell in love with—thus, the protesting ceased.

"Poloo," she cooed as I closed the door.

"What?" I growled as I worked my fingers.

"Stop," she whined while a lone tear slipped down her make-up free face.

"Do you really want me to stop?" I groaned as my dick knocked against the zipper of my pants.

Her silence was the go ahead for me to bring her to an intense orgasm. As she was close to cumming on my fingers, I pulled them out and placed her on the ground.

"What the fuck, Polo?" she hissed, erratically.

I didn't respond to her statement until after I sucked her juices off my fingers.

"Mmm, very tasty, you are. I didn't have breakfast this mornin'," I quickly spat before taking off my shirt.

With an evil eye, Cella glared at me as if she wanted to attack me—sexually. Laughing, I took a seat on the clean, black bench. Cella sighed heavily as she flung her head backwards. She was sexually frustrated. How I knew? Because she couldn't stop moaning while pressing her arms against her titties.

"Cella, you can get it if you want it? You do know that right? This dick is yo's. All you gott--," I stated before she quickly moved to a black steel dresser, plopping her ass on top of it.

Spreading her legs, showcasing a pussy that had me beating my dick at the thought of it, she cooed while toying with her hairless monkey, "You said you hadn't had breakfast ... come eat."

A motherfucker didn't have to tell me twice to hop off that damn bench. My face was planted in between Cella's wide spread legs before either of us knew it. I took my time tasting and pleasing her until she begged for me to reach into the bottom drawer to get a condom.

"What in the fuck are you doin' wit' condoms here, Cella?" I questioned angrily.

"Your crazy ass cousin is the reason why I keep condoms here," she voiced breathlessly.

As I stood erect with an ugly facial expression, Cella snickered, "That surely didn't sound right. Your cousin has been here a time or ten and taken a random broad with him. So to not cut out his time of bedding and ditching the random, he insisted that I keep condoms here for him so that he wouldn't raw dog a bitch. He said that he was a recovering raw-dogging addict whom was trying to learn protection before friction."

Shaking my head while laughing, I knew without a doubt that Cella wasn't lying. Protection before friction was the phrase that we embedded day and night into that nigga's brain for over a fucking year—some years back. We had to tell that nigga that he couldn't be out raw dogging everything that he came across. Yes, he had a problem with condoms. Thus, we had to carry extra for that idiot and ourselves. We had to have them stashed in our cars, the garage, and our homes.

"Now, can you get the condom please," Cella sexily voiced before biting on her bottom lip.

"Nawl, we gotta get on better terms than that. Now, let's get to the tattin' thing," I told her as I held out my hand for her to grab.

"You are going to fuck me right now, Polo, and I am not playing with you," she stated with an attitude.

"Oh no, I ain't gon' fuck you. You won't answer any of my calls or text; yet, you want me to give you som' of my precious dick. Oh, beautiful sweetheart, you got me all types of fucked up," I fired off with a raised eyebrow.

"You gave the *nothings* the dick. So, why not give the *something* the dick?" her smart mouthed ass inquired before standing to her feet.

Quickly continuing, she shot off, "I guess Nyko will have to do, after all."

Why in the fuck did she say that? I sure as hell didn't know but that shit pissed me the fuck off. Yet, I wasn't going to let Cella see that she ruffled my feathers—real bad.

"Can we get started on the tattoo, please?" I nicely asked as I backed towards the bench with my game face on.

"Sure thing."

Two and half hours later, I had a beautiful masterpiece on my back. Two doves were flying high towards a group of clouds that had the sun shining brightly. Inside of each of the doves' bodies were my sons' names. Cella did a great job of free-drawing my daughters' faces before placing her artwork on the lower half of my back. In the center of my back the sun rays beamed on a banner that held said love conquers all.

As I grabbed my shirt, Cella cleared her throat while standing in front of the door with her arms folded.

Enjoying her behavior, I chuckled while throwing my shirt over my head.

"You ain't going nowhere until you give me what I want," she voiced bossily.

"Woman, I did give you what you wanted. You told me to eat, an' damn it I ate," I replied as I scrolled towards her.

"Look, I'm not about to play with you about your dick sliding inside of me. So, the quicker we get on with it … the quicker you can go and enjoy the rest of your day," she announced smartly before biting on her bottom lip.

As bad as I wanted to feel every inch of her juice box, I politely declined.

"Tell me why you won't give it to me? Hell, you can fuck everyone else at the drop of a hat."

Growling, I roughly gripped her thighs and slid her ass up the door. I needed Cella to be eye to eye with me. As I gazed into her beautiful eyes, she seductively told me to fuck her up against the door.

"I won't give in to what you want 'cause you won't give in to what I want. I just don't want you as a sex toy. I want you as my woman. I just don't want to fuck an' leave you alone. I wanna sex, make love, and then fuck you followed by cuddlin' wit' you afterwards. I don't want my dick in any other's broad's mouth. I want it in yours. I want to be a one-woman's man … yo' man, Cella."

With tears streaming down her face, she softly replied, "I can't be your woman. I don't have enough faith or trust in us, Polo. I just want us to fuck whenever I want."

"Cella, if you don't have faith or trust in us … then you don't need me in between yo' legs," I voiced as I placed her on the ground.

As I opened the door, I cleared my throat. Slowly dropping my head forwards, I sighed heavily before turning around to face the woman that I knew I could spend the rest of my life with.

"You deserve more than just a roll 'round in the bed. I can't give you that an' walk out of yo' home or let you walk down my stairs. I'm sorry I can't. You take it easy, Cella."

CHAPTER EIGHTEEN
Cella

Normally, I would be at Bama Lanes with my girls—enjoying happy hour and three rounds of bowling; however, I wasn't in tune with their positive, enthusiastic attitude. I was extremely sad that my promising love life went to shits in a matter of seconds last month. I thought Polo and I were going to make a great team. I just knew that he was going to be the only man that I would allow to be inside of me.

As I pushed Polo out of my mind, I focused on my sorry ass baby daddy and whether he received word about me seeking full custody of Xyla. He hadn't called or texted since the day he thought I was going to bond his ass out of jail, which I knew was going to happen. The day I found enough courage to file for full custody was the day I let those that didn't love and respect my daughter and me go. I had to wash my hands with them. They weren't good for Xyla, and they sure as well wasn't good for me.

Ring. Ring. Ring.

My thoughts ceased as I rolled over to grab my ringing cellphone. Placing my eyes on the screen, I saw LaJuan's name.

Rolling my eyes as I smacked my lips, I calmly answered the phone—for the final time.

"Hello."

"Cella," he softly stated in a sad tone.

"What?"

"I'm sorry," he cried.

With a raised eyebrow and a smirk on my face, "What do you want, LaJuan?"

"I just wanted to say that I'm sorry for being a sucky dad and a horrible boyfriend to you. You were good to me, Cella. You were and still is a good woman."

"Hmm, mmm. Now, what is the real nature of this call?" I stated smartly as images of Polo and I crept into my mind.

I wonder what he's doing.

"I want to be in my daughter's life. There shouldn't be a reason I'm not involved in hers as I am with my other children," he stated sniffling.

My dumb ass sperm donor had my thoughts of Polo cut off with his statement. I laughed. As I did so, he asked me what was so funny.

"You are nigga! You are!" I loudly voiced before continuing, "You must got served those lovely papers?"

"Yes."

"Um, so sign them. You have never did anything for her. No matter how many times I try to trust you, you find a way to fuck shit up. I'm done. You can be free to do as you please without hurting my daughter. This shit has gone on for eight longgg motherfucking years. For years, I let you escape without doing your duties for *our* daughter. You've let me do everything for Xyla, and I prayed that you would step in and be a real father to her like you are to those other children of yours. Your sorry ass couldn't call and tell our daughter happy birthday or purchase her anything. You are free motherfucker," I voiced happily as I couldn't wait to have his name off my daughter's birth certificate.

"Cella, can we make some type of arrangements ... like child support or ... or something else?"

I had to burst out laughing at that stupid ass nigga's question.

"I'm serious, Cella."

"This parenting thing is not about money, LaJuan. This is about you being a father to Xyla. I can't keep letting you slide without slanging a hot ass bullet into your ass. Before I risk my freedom over your nothing, deadbeat ass ... I rather dismiss your ass out of her life like you have been doing since the day I told you I was pregnant."

"Cella, I will pay child support," he begged.

Chuckling, I replied, "Why? So, you can boast and down-talk about me as if I'm this and I'm that? You do know who you are talking to right? The *bitch* whom owns a tattoo shop and work on exclusive cars. So, you know I am not going for that skit gone wrong shit you are talking about, LaJuan. Sign the damn papers. You have three days or I will bring the fucking heat down on your ass!"

"You ain't got no heat to bring down on me," he replied, revealing the real LaJuan Nixon.

"Boy, I know you fucking that little fast ass fourteen year old girl that stay over there by Vanice. I saw your nasty dick ass creeping out of that girl's bedroom window when her mother came home. I got photos to show anyone, especially the authorities. Don't sign those papers and see how you will be labeled as a pedophile or a rapist," I voiced quickly before telling a strong faced lie. "I'll let the court decide; especially with the latest shit that Vanice recorded y'all doing."

In a low tone, he replied, "I'll have it signed by tomorrow and mailed back in."

"Nice doing business with you, Mr. LaJuan Nixon," I stated in a business timbre before hanging the phone up.

"Well, damn. Now, I wonder what type of shit he did with the girl," I voiced as I placed my phone on the pillow.

Ring. Ring. Ring.

I knew LaJuan wasn't responsible for my line ringing, especially after I put him on blast about the fourteen year old girl he was messing around with. I secretly hoped it was Polo calling. I was disappointed when I saw Sunny's name on the display screen.

"Hello," I voiced casually.

"We are on the way to cheer you up," she stated as the others chimed in.

Not wanting to be bothered, I had to come up with a quick lie. "No need to come over."

"And why the fuck not?" Ke'Lena voiced loudly.

"Because I am not home," I lied.

"Well, where in the fuck are you?" my girls asked in unison.

Chuckling, I rapidly announced, "Now, that isn't any of your business."

Before they got a chance to respond, I ended the call. I be damned if they didn't call me back; I didn't answer.

My phone rang once more; this time it was my brother.

"What's up?" I greeted him.

"Shit. Coolin'. I was callin' to check on you."

"I'm doing okay. How about yourself?"

"Good," he quickly voiced before continuing, "Have you heard about the latest shit our sister did?"

"Nope," I replied as I stared at the muted T.V.

"Let's just say that she got outted on social media. Apparently, she doesn't know who got her ass pregnant."

"Whoa. Explain?" I snickered as I shook my head.

"So she told us at the cabin that Polo was responsible for her an' Joana being pregnant, right?"

"Yeah."

"Well, she told three other niggas they were the father too."

"You gotta be shitting me," I voiced as I sat upright in the bed.

"Nope. Those comments are a motherfucker. They shamed her ass somethin' awful to the point her dumb ass deactivated her account."

"Well, damn. I feel sorry for that baby that's gonna come out of that twat."

"Me too. Mom an' Dad are pissed off."

"Of course they are. They will have to raise the child."

"Same thing they said."

We chatted well over an hour before he asked me what was up with Polo and me. I told him the truth. What my brother said to me had me thinking on another level. I took heed to what he had to say; however, I still felt the way that I felt or should I say what I had trained myself to feel about us being in a relationship. If I couldn't get on demand dick, then I didn't want to be with Polo like that.

"Cella, he didn't know that you an' Traneice are sisters. He's human, Cella. He was goin' through somethin' that no parent should ever have to go through. Give him a raincheck on him dissin' you fo' some deep throated, wide open pussy females. He told you why he left. Would you have liked the way he treated you if he hadn't left?"

"No."

"Okay, then. Iron things out. If he really isn't what you want, at least you gave y'all a fair chance without any extra bullshit."

Sighing sharply, I replied, "Why won't you give love and relationships another try?"

"Because I am not ready for it, Cella … you know this."

"It seems like you need to give love and relationships another chance as well, don't you big brother?"

"In due time. In due time," he huffed before telling me to hold on.

As I held on, I thought about the one chick that almost destroyed my brother's way of thinking—Tahlia Franklin. They were middle school sweethearts. He asked her to marry him when they graduated high school. She said yes. Oh, my big brother was so happy. Then, at the dinner rehearsal he was crushed upon learning that Tahlia had been sleeping with two of his friends since junior high school. My brother never saw relationships for himself in the same positive light ever since.

"I'm back," Joshua replied, snapping me into reality.

"You better be glad I didn't feel like hanging up the phone, Joshua," I spat as I held a strong smirk on my face.

Laughing, he responded, "Same ole Cella. Won't hold no longer than fifteen seconds.

My brother made sure to end our conversation with positive vibes. That was one thing that I could count on from him. He made sure to let me know that I deserved to be happy because I was a good person. If there wasn't a soul rooting for me, my brother damn sure was. He's my go-to person for anything, bad or good. There wasn't a thing in this world that we couldn't discuss. We had a bond that Traneice hated with a passion. I never understood why; hell, we grew up in the same house. The thought of Traneice caused me to become angry; thus, I ceased thoughts about her treacherous ass.

Sighing heavily, I decided that I needed a bottle of wine and some R&R in the tub filled with bubbles and scented candles as acid jazz played at a nice decibel from the radio in my room. Hopping away from my bed, I ambled towards the kitchen. Along the way, I thought of the good times I had with Polo. My favorite time with him was when we were at my lake house. With a smile on my face at the nice time we had together, I grabbed the bottle of sparkly, sweet wine.

Jogging up the stairs, my heart told me where I should be but my mind wasn't hearing any of that shit. Quickly opening the wine, I guzzled a nice amount as I turned on the radio, selecting my favorite acid jazz cd. Pleased with the mood that I was setting for myself, I sashayed towards the newly decorated black, red, and silver themed bathroom. I was eager to sit my confused ass in the large garden tub that had six jets that would eject the much needed hot, bubbly water.

As I turned on the tub's knobs, my heart spoke loud and clear. This time I couldn't ignore it. My breath was taken away every time I tried to deter my mind. Knowing where I had to be, I quickly cancelled the thought of having a relaxing bath. Instead, I turned on the showerhead followed by rapidly stripping out of my bra, panties, and socks. I couldn't pretend that I was okay with the decision of solely fucking Polo whenever I wanted. I wasn't okay with not being around him, and giving us a fair shot. It seemed as if I was torturing myself so that I wouldn't get hurt by him. I had to do what my girls, my parents, brother, and heart said — to give him a fair chance so that I really know if we were meant to be.

Twenty minutes later, I was dressed in a tank top and jogging shorts. My shoes were laced as I snatched my phone and the keys to Tealy. Running down the stairs, I made sure that my back, side, and front doors were locked. While aiming for the garage door, my front doorbell sounded off.

Turning around, I yelled, "Who is it?"

"Polo."

My eyes were wide as a huge grin was on my face. My heart was racing as I was eager to open the door. My limbs shook uncontrollably as I couldn't wait to be in his arms. My soul was leaving my body, ready to become one with him. That was until my mind started fucking with me.

The moment I opened the door, Polo snatched me up and placed his wet face to mine. His wet, puffy eyes got the best of me.

"I need you, Cella. Please don't shut me out. Whatever you want me to do, I will do it."

"Make love to me, Madison. Spend the night with me, Madison. Don't ever lie or keep anything from me, Madison. Most importantly, I need you too, Madison. But, I'm scared ... like really really scared and confused," I cooed as I looked into his glossy eyes.

"Say my name once more, beautiful," he voiced sweetly as he closed and locked the door.

"Madison," I stated as two long tears dripped down my face.

"Your wish is my command," he announced before walking to my room.

***

Our lovemaking was splendid. I had a smile on my face that couldn't be wiped off. Polo opened himself up the moment he fed me grapes, cubed cheese, and deli-cut meats. I learned what happened between him, Janah, and Nyko—in full detail. Now, I knew why he had so much hatred for the deceased mother of his deceased sons. Polo's love ran deep when it concerned

Janah. Then, she destroyed it by betraying him. That's where his need for using females came in—sex. The moment Polo placed his eyes on me I deterred him of his plan of not falling for another woman. He was quick to tell me that he was stupid for thinking that he needed to stay away from me.

Afterwards, our conversations shifted towards his daughters then it moved to what he wanted out of life. He made it clear that he wanted Xyla and me in it. I didn't say that I wanted to be in his life, but he knew that I did. What was understood didn't need to be explained on my part.

Next, we discussed my sister and Joana. That topic was clear cut. He used them for threesomes and that he never slept with either of them raw. The only thing that I could think of was that Traneice really liked Polo, and that she was willing to do anything for him—in hopes that he would see her in a different light and make her his.

"Now, we have talked 'bout me enough, woman. I want to know why do Traneice hates you so much?"

"I have no idea. We grew up in the same home, of course. I don't know why she feels such strong negative emotions towards me."

"Have you asked her?"

"How many times have our parents, my brother, and I have asked her why she dislikes me? Every time she would say in a smug tone that she doesn't dislike me."

"Is there somethin' that you have accomplished that she hasn't? Was there a guy that she liked but the dude didn't like her? School accomplishments?" he asked while rubbing my backside.

"No to none of it."

"You think it might be just simple yet dumb hatred fo' you?"

I nodded my head. I've never done anything for my sister to dislike or disown me. I was always there for Traneice even when she wasn't there for me. It had been that way since she been in this world. Joshua, Traneice, and I weren't that far apart in age. So, it wasn't like one child got treated better than the other. We received the same treatment. When one got in trouble, all of us did.

Ring. Ring. Ring.

My phone interrupted our conversation. With my phone in my hand, I pondered what my sister wanted. That heifer never called me in the dead of the morning — two o'clock to be exact.

"Hello," I voiced as I snuggled closer into Polo's warm, muscular arm.

"Cella, I need you. My car broke down," Traneice stated in a scared timbre.

Sitting upright, I said, "Where are you?"

"On Narrow Lane Road, passed Red Lion Apartments and the old club that was called the Diamond."

"You talking about the extremely dark part?" I inquired as I hopped out of the bed.

"Yes."

"You don't have towing assistance on your car to get it to a shop?" I asked as I quickly ran to the dresser that housed my jogging pants and plain V-neck shirts.

"No. Couldn't afford all that extra shit."

"Okay. I'll be there in a minute."

"Okay. Thank you," she replied softly yet sincerely.

"No problem," I replied before the call ended.

"What's wrong?" Polo questioned as he stood, putting on his clothes.

"Traneice's car broke down on Narrow Lane Road … in the dark spot."

"A'ight. I'm goin'."

As I put on my clothing, I told him that he should stay here. The last thing I needed was for them to be arguing and shit. My job was simple—assist her ass, followed by shipping her home or wherever she was trying to get too.

"You don't need to be out there alone. We are in Murkgomery in case you forgot. These niggas don't give a damn about robbing a female."

I hated when people called the city Murkgomery—even though, niggas did complete a lot of killing.

"I know. I will be careful. I keep that tool on me at all times," I told him as I slipped my feet into the latest pair of Jordan's.

"I'm comin' wit' you," he insisted as he grabbed his gun and cellphone from the dresser.

"No. I'll talk to you the entire way there, and while I'm there. Stay. Don't feel like dealing with Traneice shit talking."

"Then, why are you helpin' her?"

"Because my parents told us that no matter what if family seeks help then we must help."

"I'm goin' wit' you, Cella," he replied sternly.

"I said no. Now, the longer we go back and forth about this … the longer it takes for me to get back into our comfortable position."

Sighing heavily, he nodded his head before saying, "Okay."

Skipping away from my bedroom, down the stairs, into the garage, I couldn't wait until I was back in my safe haven. I wasn't the type to be out of my home if I wasn't with my girls. Before I hopped into my Range Rover, Polo asked could he come with me. Of course, I told him no. Before I left my street, he was calling my phone.

As we talked on the phone, I felt warm and fuzzy. The light conversation that we indulged in made me want to turn around and abandoned my sister like she did my daughter and me; yet, my mother didn't instill in us to do dirt for dirt.

Traneice was fifteen minutes away from my home, but I had it in my mind that I wanted to be there within ten minutes; thus, I drove rapidly all the while thankful that no police officers were ducked off in the dark areas of the back road, I choose travel down.

The closer I got to the place, the quicker I was ready to help my bird brain sister out. With my high beams on, I saw my sister's dark blue Chevy Cobalt on the side of the road. Bypassing my sister's car, I made an illegal U-turn in the road. Shortly afterwards, I parked my car in front of hers.

Before I jumped out of my vehicle, I made sure that my gun had a bullet in the chamber. Polo was in my ear talking nasty causing me to blush.

"Hush up, sir," I told him as Traneice stepped out of the car.

"Hey, thanks fo' comin' out to help me."

"No problem. What did your car do?" I asked while walking towards the driver's door.

"It just shut down. No warning. I'm sittin' on on a full tank of gas," she replied.

Instantly, I knew she was lying. The car was parked too perfectly to have shut down. As I slowly turned around, my sister was too close upon me.

"Get her truck! I will bring her ass to the place that we discussed earlier! Go gown Narrow Lane Road like I told you too!" Traneice yelled.

As I saw two people dressed in all-black with a ski-mask over their faces, Polo yelled in my ear, "I told yo' ass I should've come wit' you!"

By the time he said the word you, I felt the worst pain sear through the left side of my body.

"Ahhh!" I screamed at the same time my SUV skirted off in the direction my sister demanded.

"I'm not too far from you Cella," he rushed into the phone before saying something that was inaudible due to Traneice loudly talking in my face.

"I want you dead, Cella. You always steal the light from me. I want your ass in a casket. Oh, don't worry about Xyla, her spoiled ass will be loved … that is until I cease her from breathing in her sleep," my sister stated as an American muscle zipped passed up.

VJ.

The mentioning of my daughter dying at the hands of the bitch that cared less for us brought upon the beast that I never wanted to show anyone. With as much force as I could muster, I kneed my sister in the stomach before reaching for my gun. I didn't get a chance to get it. Two bullets ripped through my body, causing me to scream out and drop to the ground. A searing pain graced my abdomen and right leg with such force that I couldn't block out the pain.

This can't be it. I can't leave my daughter behind.

The moment four shots rang out, my sister and the motherfucker that shot me fell to the ground. My sister yelped as the other person didn't. Loud speakers blasted, playing the only song that brought tears to my face as I began to panic.

Blood was gushing out of the wounds as the pain wouldn't let up on my ass no matter what I tried to think about.

Polo.

"I do love you," one of the guys from GQ stated loudly. Tears seeped down my face as I knew my situation was not a good one. Thus, I began to pray for the safety of my child, and the strength my family and friends would need to have upon my fate.

"My baby, I love you soooo," the singers from GQ stated even more loudly from the speakers that I personally tweaked for my benefit.

He surely love that car. Hopefully, my parents and Joshua will give it to him ... if I don't.

At the sight of high beamed lights, my body relaxed as my mind stopped thinking—followed by my eyelids closing--involuntarily.

CHAPTER NINETEEN
Polo

Friday, July 13th

The moment Cella left out of the house, I was on the phone with VJ. It was a good damn thing I knew where Traneice fuck ass had my girl going, and that VJ wasn't in a fucking spree with Crystal. If not, shit was going to get real ugly in the city of Montgomery. There wasn't going to be a motherfucker in the State of Alabama that could tell me any fucking thing.

I badly wanted to tell VJ to kill Traneice. Yet, that wouldn't be good enough for her ass. I wanted to see that bitch in prison where I was going to take pleasure in controlling how her day was going to be for as long as the State of Alabama was going to keep her ass in their prison system.

"What is taking them so long to update us on the well-being of my child?" Cella's mother inquired as two police officers and another individual that wasn't dressed in police uniform strolled our way.

Cella's girls' comforted Mrs. Dorsey as Joshua, Mr. Dorsey, VJ, and I stood to greet the officers. The fellas kept Xyla occupied as they played several rounds of Go Fish with her. They kept her supplied with food and drinks. Basically, they kept her out of the way in case we received bad news.

"Jessie," the baldheaded White man dressed in plain clothing stated as he extended out his hand to Mr. Dorsey.

"Wayne," Mr. Dorsey stated as they shook hands—firmly.

"You asked for me?" Wayne inquired.

"Can we speak in private?" Mr. Dorsey questioned.

"We don't need to speak at all. I was quickly brought to speed about what happened to your daughters. Rest assured that everything will go as I think you want it to go, sir," Wayne replied calmly.

"What do you think I want to happen?"

"That no one is arrested but your daughter Traneice for the murder of three individuals on top of possible robbery attempt. To have an inaccurate report submitted."

"Very well. When will this take place?"

"It already has. The moment the hospital clears Traneice my guys will arrest her."

"Very well then," Mr. Dorsey voiced as he extended his hand. "Thank you, Wayne."

"What did I tell you about thanking me? If it wasn't for you, my brother and I wouldn't be alive to start a family of our own.

We owe you for life, and we meant that," Wayne stated genuinely before looking at the two semi-young officers beside him.

Quickly, I read their badges. Their last names were McArthur.

"Jessie, meet my son Jessie and my brother's son Joseph," Wayne voiced proudly.

The guys shook hands and said nice pleasantries.

Shortly afterwards, Wayne spoke to his family members, "This heroic man is the very reason y'all are here on this earth. If he hadn't risked his own life to pull my brother and me out of a burning building overseas, we would've died. If he didn't have the guts to say screw what his platoon leader ordered, then we wouldn't have been here. This man is the person that you must thank him every time you see him. If he needs anything, you must be there for him and his family. Understood?"

"Yes, sir," they announced in unison.

"The family of Marcella Dorsey!" a woman loudly voiced from the right of us.

In a flash, we were standing in front of a chunky woman that held a blank facial expression.

"She's stable. Her vitals are good," was all that I cared to hear before I began thanking God.

The only thing that brought me out of my trance was hearing Sunny ask, "Um, run that by us again, please."

"Ms. Dorsey, loss the pregnancy," the chunky nurse voiced softly.

"Pregnancy?" I heard everyone state as I came to.

"We didn't know that she was. Are you sure?" I voiced with a raised eyebrow.

"Yes, her blood work determined that. She was freshly pregnant like close to five weeks."

Nashville when we were doing all that fucking.

A nurse's name was called over the intercom, ceasing the nurse from talking to us. The moment the intercom was cut off she sweetly said, "Your loved one is a strong woman. A very determined and vicious fighter. She will be fine. My prayers will continue to soar for you guys and her. God bless."

Two hours later, we were in a semi-cold private room glaring at Cella as she was sedated. The beeping of the machines caused me to feel numb as a thought seeped into my mind, causing me to fear that things would turn out for the worse. I did something that I rarely did in the wee hours of the morning — call my parents and asked for them to come to the hospital so that they could pray over my Cella.

***

It was well in the afternoon when Cella's eyes opened. I was the first one that she saw; I was lying in the bed with her.

"Hey, you," I voiced softly before I placed a kiss on her lips.

"I told your ass to stay at *home*, Polo," she voiced with a weak smile on her face.

She put emphasis on home causing me to wonder did she intentionally say it, or was her memory slipping.

Not in the mood to question it, I said, "You know I'm hardheaded. So, I couldn't stay at *home*."

"Thank you," she breathed slowly as everyone surrounded the bed.

Several 'hey you's, 'thank god she's woke', and 'I love you's' seeped out of their mouths, creating a perfect song just for her.

"I was getting ready to jump on the bed to wake you up, like I did when we were younger," Joshua joked as he placed a kiss on Cella's forehead.

As we laughed at him, there were two knocks strategically placed on the door before it was opened. As we turned to see who it was, loud gasps left several of their mouths as I glared at the one bitch I wished I could've killed — Traneice.

"Thank you for bringing her in here," Mr. Dorsey stated in a stern tone.

"No problem, sir," one of the uniformed officers replied before bringing Traneice closer towards Cella.

Immediately, I was in defense mode for the woman that I had grown to adore within two months.

"Traneice, what you have done was uncalled for. You attacked your sister in the worst way possible. You cost her to lose a life that she was going to bring into this wor--," Mr. Dorsey stated before Cella weakly said what.

"You were pregnant honey," Mrs. Dorsey's soothing voice replied as she looked at her daughter.

With a blank facial expression, Cella spoke low as her eyes spoke high.

"You are dead to me, Traneice. You were going to kill the one person that loved you more than anyone in this room, my daughter. For that, I hope you get everything you deserve in life. You should be glad that I can't move how I want right now because I would kill you with my bare hands, and I'm very sure no one in this room would stop me. You are going to enjoy prison. Since that's where you are going to be until …

hopefully, you die. I hope the people that you had killed because you wanted me dead haunts you every single day and night."

"You are on your own, now, Traneice. I will pay for no lawyers to be on your team. Your father and I will not put any money on your books. I hope your hatred for your sister was worth you being isolated and on your own," Mrs. Dorsey stated in a tone that led me to believe that she was fed up.

"Take her away," Mr. Dorsey ordered.

Just like that, the bitch was being carried off while whining and begging her parents to forgive her and not turn their backs on her. The room went quiet as we glared at Cella whom was looking at me. The look in her eyes told me that she was scared.

"I'm not goin' anywhere, woman, and neither is Xyla. She's wit' her other grandparents visitin' the vendin' machines."

"Yassss," Cella's girls' stated happily in unison.

Oddly, Cella asked, "Other grandparents?"

"His parents' guh. His … parents' … guh. Now, don't wake up actin' all slow an' stuff," Crystal voiced happily before winking her eye and blowing Cella a kiss.

"Is that so, huh?" Cella asked before yawning.

"Very much so," VJ replied as he placed two small teal and gold boxes onto Cella's stomach.

"Nih, wait a whole minute ... is he ... is he," Crystal stated as I slid out of the bed and dropped to my knees.

"Ohh, shoot, he is," Cella's girls' stated in an excited timbre as Cella placed her beautiful moist eyes on me.

"Marcella Nicole Dorsey, we have known each other fo' a short amount of time, but that doesn't stop me from wantin' to be wit' you an' Xyla every second of the day. I, Madison Marcell Willis, promise to treat an' love you an' Xyla wit' much respect an' love. I promise to never leave y'all side as long as I'm on this earth. So, I've been told by Tyanna that you are not one fo' one too many spontaneous actions in a row ... so I had to change my original plan. Wit' that being said, would you do me the honor of bein' my woman first before I hold you in my arms as we jump the broom?" I asked sincerely as I glared at the most gorgeous woman in the world as tears seeped down her face as she nodded her head.

Pulling myself up, I rushed my lips to hers. Those damn fireworks popped off the moment she sucked my tongue into her hot ass mouth.

Quickly, I broke the kiss off.

While laughing, I said, "Now, we gotta do somethin' 'bout that hot breath of yours like as of now. No more kissin' 'til I brush your mouth."

The laughter and jokes filled the room until my parents and Xyla strolled in with happy facial expressions.

"Mommy, you are woke!" Xyla breathed excitedly as tears welled in her beautiful brown eyes.

"I am. I am. Hi gorgeous," Cella spoke as I scooped Xyla into my arms.

Leaning down to kiss her mother, Xyla told Cella that she loved her.

"I love you more, Duda Byrd," Cella's soft tone stated before yawning.

"You need to rest, Mommy."

Chuckling, Cella replied, "Yes, Ma'am, Nurse Xyla."

Placing her eyes on me, Xyla asked me, "Sooo, have you asked her to marry you yet?"

"Not yet. I did ask her to be my girlfriend."

"Ouu, what did she say?" she asked eagerly.

"She said yes," I smiled.

As Xyla hugged me tightly, I couldn't understand why she was excited about her mom and I dating when she didn't know me or hadn't been around me long enough to like me.

"Xyla, I have a two questions fo' you," I announced in a fatherly tone.

"Yes, sir."

"Why do you want yo' mom an' me together?"

"Because you are just right for her as she is just right for you."

"And how do you know that?" the adults asked in unison.

"Well, because all y'all have said so. So, since y'all are way older than me, I thought hey maybe the adults know what they are talking about. Plus, the way that you and mommy look at each other was a way that my dad and mommy never looked at each other," she voiced softly.

"She is going to be a private investigator or a detective or something," my father stated with a chuckle, causing everyone else to chuckle and agree with him.

"Well, wit' that being said Xyla," I told her as I placed her on the ground.

I grabbed the box off Cella's stomach before bending on one knee.

"Xyla Nicole Dorsey, we barely know each other yet I feel that it's only right to ask fo' yo' hand in a promise so that I, Madison Marcell Willis, can be the father figure that you need in yo' life. Not only as yo' mother's rock but yours as well. I promise to love, respect, an' treat you as if you are my own. Will you take my ring an' become my daughter, Xyla?"

With a huge smile on her face, she hugged me tightly before throwing out her right hand followed by saying, "Bim."

"I don't know what we gonna do wit' her," Joshua laughed while we laughed at Xyla's reaction to have the ring placed on her finger.

The rest of our day and night went smoothly the moment I sent everyone home. Softly rubbing my sleeping beauty's face, I remembered what she told me the night that caused me to give her all of me. Placing my mouth to her ear, I recited the words—remixed a little—that she said to me, and I meant every damn word!

"You are just like me, an' it scares me. You are someone that I truly never had in my life, outside of my parents an' kids, an' that scares me. I'm doin' the unthinkable, an' that scares me too but I'm not goin' to regret givin' you all of me 'cause I feel that you need all of me."

CHAPTER TWENTY
Cella

Thursday, September 13th

Recovery was a bitch in a handbasket. My abdomen and leg pains weren't as severe as before; yet, it was still bothersome. However, I had to work out the kinks in them so that I could return to the full throttle Cella that I was before the ambush. After the first day of walking up and down those damn stairs in my house, I had to tell Polo that I preferred sleeping downstairs. He agreed; thus, he camped out in the front room with me as well. No matter when I had the slightest pain, Polo was right there by my side. He was so far underneath me that I had to tell him to go out and have fun with the fellas. Oh, no he wasn't hearing that shit; that damn man brought the party to me so that I wouldn't be out of his eyesight.

Xyla and I thought it was best to expedite Polo moving into the large estate that I owned off Taylor Road—commonly known as the party house. Instantly, the fellas helped Polo move his furniture into a storage shed as he brought his clothes and things of that nature to my house. Plus, I was tired of him having to leave to retrieve clothes and shit.

My doctor had me on light duty. There weren't so many things that I could do as far as working. I didn't work on cars, but I did simple tatts—ones that would take no longer than forty-five minutes. I wasn't open six days a week for the time being. Polo thought it was best for me to be open three days a week with an opening time at nine a.m. and closing time at noon. Of course, I disagreed yet my girls and the fellas were on his side. I was outnumbered. I took what I could.

Ring. Ring. Ring.

Picking up my phone off the floor, I saw my brother's name displaying on the screen.

Quickly, I answered.

"Happy birthday, jughead guh," he sang happily.

"Thank you." I smiled.

"How's the birthday guh, feelin'?"

"Good and doped up." I laughed.

"That's what's up. Xyla off to school?"

Ever since school started back last month, Polo took it upon himself to take and pick up Xyla. That man wouldn't let me do anything, not even put a pad inside of my period panties. The look on my face when he offered to stick a tampon in my coochie was beyond priceless. I couldn't scream loud enough for him to get the hell out of the bathroom. He was truly a wonderful gift, and I thanked the Man above day and night for Polo not fighting what was destined for us to have.

"Yes, she's off with a huge smile on her face."

Chuckling, Joshua replied, "Tell Polo I said what's up."

"I will when he returns. They left fifteen minutes ago."

"They left out late."

"Yep because Polo's ass decided that he wanted to cook a huge breakfast this morning," I spoke with a smile on my face.

"Well damn," my brother stated rapidly before continuing, "I just wanted to call you before I go into this courtroom. The arraignment will start soon. I wanna know what this broad going to say."

"Oh. Well, I'm sure Traneice will not cease to amaze you. I'm ready to lie down for a while. My med are kicking in. I will talk to you later on, k?" I told him, rushing to get off the phone with him. I cared less about the child our parents made.

"Okay. Rest up an' I love you."

"Me love you more, Joshua."

As we ended the call, I exhaled as I dropped my phone on the floor. Like the cartoon head that I was, I was logged into the T.V. as *Fish Hooks* held my attention. Bea and Milo were two fish that kept me well entertained until I overheard the low growl of Tealy. Excitedly, I slowly sat upright on the sofa — eager to greet my man.

Shortly afterwards, the sexiest voiced man loudly stated while waltzing into our cool home. "Whatever it is, it don't matter, I'll pay the shippin' costs."

"Ah, I see someone is enjoying the hell out Tealy and Ronnie Bell's song," I laughed as I slowly lifted off the sofa.

"Sat cho ass down, woman. I'm comin' to you," he spat in an authoritative tone.

"Yes, sir," I cooed in a slurred tone.

"Ole high ass," he replied as he kneeled in front of me, placing a kiss on my lips.

"And I'm getting a little hot and bothered down there," I hissed as I placed his hand on my kitty cat.

"After the fuckin' fiasco that took place early this mornin' … nawl, I'm good love," he spat seriously causing me to laugh.

"Polo, it wasn't like I meant to do it. I was still slightly doped up and had minimal control," I laughed.

"And yo' ass damn near doped up now. So, like I said before I'm good," he replied while taking a seat next to me.

"I smelled like roses and peaches huh?" I joked while laughing.

"Yo' ass smelled like pure baby shit, Cella. That damn fart just took me out the game. How in the hell can you be so damn beautiful an' then turn 'round an' drop a fuckin' wet ass, ugly ass fart like that? What in the fuck did you eat last night?" he inquired as I was in tears laughing at him.

"Everythin' I had the munchies for," I snickered.

"Well, tonight put in an order fo' fruits only, please. At least I know tonight I will have a better chance at survivin' if you fart."

"Aye, aye, Captain."

"So, my woman, I don't think you are gettin' Tealy back. I'm goin' to make her mine," he stated in a matter-of-fact tone.

"Oh hell to the no, I don't think so. However, we can share her ... from time to time," I replied with a smile on my face before I kissed him.

"That sounds like a plan ... I guess," he quickly replied before continuing, "If you are offerin' to share Tealy wit' me, I know the birthday woman feelin' good today."

"Actually, I'm more than good. I'm blessed and highly favored," I told him as my house phone and cellphone rang.

"Mm, I think I'm the one that's really blessed and highly favored," he voiced softly before he initiated a passionate kiss between us.

As my body began to tingle, I laid back as I tried to pull Polo on top of me. With a raised eyebrow, he shook his head followed by mouthing no. While I sighed heavily from him refusing to satisfy my hungry coochie, my phones stopped ringing.

"It's time to walk 'round fo' ten minutes," he stated as he stood, followed by extending his hand.

As I placed my hand in his, I said, "Yes, it is."

"Want to go outside?" he asked as our phones began to ring again.

"No. In here is fine," I replied as he answered his phone all the while bending to retrieve mine.

Seeing my Mom's name on the display screen, I shook my head at him. I made a mental note to call her later. I didn't want to talk to anyone but Polo.

"A'ight. Let me know," he stated in the phone before ending the call.

"Traneice's arraignment is today. You aren't goin' … still?"

"Nope. Next subject please," I stated politely as I began walking around the front room.

"What do you want to do fo' yo' birthday?"

"Practice on makin' another baby." I shot off seriously.

"Um, when you are fully healed we can."

"Nope. You asked me what I wanted to do for my birthday, and I told you so it's only right for you to fulfill that, Madison Marcell Willis," I voiced in a boss-like manner.

To ensure that he caught my drift, I called him by his full government name as I looked him directly in the eyes.

"Well, shit, now Marcella Nicole Dorsey, I guess a nigga gotta get wit' it huh?" he voiced as he grabbed my hand.

"Yep."

"Alright after our ten minute walking session, we shower then we get to it," he growled sexily.

"Indeed," I responded as I toyed with my tongue.

"Fuck that, we finna get started now. Don't do shit you ain't got no business doin', Cella," he voiced as he picked me up, carrying me as if we were about to jump the broom.

"I'll try," I cooed as I looked into the eyes that showed nothing but pure love for me.

***

Now, I knew why Polo said that he was going to help the medicine keep me sleep longer than three hours. My home was turned into a beautiful, gold, black, and pink themed party zone for my thirty-third birthday. I knew who all had a hand in it; thus, I thanked every last person down to the children.

Several photo booths were placed throughout the front room and living room. The dining area was setup to perfection as I knew that was the main place we would be. Each table had its designated items placed on it. A beverage table for the adults displayed quite a few liquor bottles as Sunny's special made concoction sat in the middle. There was a table for non-alcoholic beverages. The treat table had me smiling from ear to ear as I didn't know which crazy friend of mine had the idea of placing a goody bag at a grown woman's party. To the left and right side of the dining room were two eight feet long tables that had tons of food nicely placed in pink plastic dishes. A breathtaking cake sat not far from the large window. I didn't know if we were supposed to eat the damn thing or just look at it.

"Happy birthday to you. Happy birthday to you," my family sang as I had a smile on my face as wide as the Pacific Ocean.

The moment they finished singing, we dug into the food and talked. As I looked around my home, it was filled with so much love from the fellas, my girls, our parents, my brother, and our children that I had tears seeping down my smiling face.

"Baby, what's wrong?" Polo asked as he grabbed my hand.

"Nothing. Nothing at all. I have the perfect family, and I wouldn't trade any of y'all for nothing in the world. Y'all are the reasons why I focus on getting better instead of focusing on what a close relative did to me. I deeply love each and every one of you," I voiced sincerely and happily as I looked my family and new family members into their faces.

"We love you too," they replied in unison.

For the next two hours, I enjoyed every conversation, hug, and kiss on the cheek. I was ready to retire for the evening; hence, I told Polo that I was tired.

"You gotta open yo' gifts then I will make the announcement that you are tired."

"Okay," I replied while yawning.

Within five minutes, I was opening gifts left and right as I sent out my thanks. Tons of cards were in my lap as I read every one of them. My girls said that I couldn't open my gifts since they weren't kid friendly; instantly, the adults and I laughed. Only their asses would get me naughty shit for my birthday, which Polo and I were going to put to full use.

"Last but not least," Polo stated as he kneeled in front of me with a sneaky look on his face while placing a large and a small bag on my lap.

"I wonder what did *my* Polo get me," I smiled before biting on my bottom lip as I gazed into his eyes while pulling out a small gold and black box.

As I opened the box, nothing was in it. When I raised my eyes to him, I saw the most gorgeous gold ring a woman could ever place her eyes on.

"We have been datin' fo' two months, so I think it's time fo' me to seal the deal on you. Xyla received her ring this mornin'. Now, it's yo' turn. Marcella Nicole Dorsey, will you--," Polo stated before I cut him off.

"Bim," I happily stated as I held out my left hand. I was extremely eager to receive that damn ring by the one man I couldn't live without.

"You an' Xyla wit' that bim," Joshua chuckled as everyone laughed, including the children while they clapped.

"Right," Tyanna laughed as Ponytail held onto her tightly.

Without further ado, Polo slid the ring on my finger as we brought our heads together. I kissed his nose, forehead, followed by landing a juicy kiss on his lips, and together we wholeheartedly said, "You are just like me, an' it scares me. You are someone that I truly never had in my life, outside of my parents an' kids, an' that scares me. I'm doin' the unthinkable, an' that scares me too but I'm not goin' to regret givin' you all of me 'cause I feel that you need all of me."

ABOUT THE AUTHOR

TN Jones resides in the state of Alabama with her daughter. Growing up, TN Jones always had a passion for and writing, which led her to writing short stories.

In 2015, TN Jones began working on her first book, *Disloyal: Revenge of a Broken Heart*, which was previously titled, *Passionate Betrayals*.

TN Jones will write in the following genres: Women's Fiction, Mystery/Suspense, Urban Fiction/Romance, Dark Erotica/Erotica, and Urban/Interracial Paranormal.

Published novels by TN Jones: *Disloyal: Revenge of a Broken Heart, Disloyal 2-3: A Woman's Revenge, A Sucka in Love for a*

Thug, If You'll Give Me Your Heart 1-2, By Any Means: Going Against the Grain 1-2, The Sins of Love: Finessing the Enemies 1-3, Caught Up In a D-Boy's Illest Love 1-3, Choosing To Love A Lady Thug 1-4, Is This Your Man, Sis: Side Piece Chronicles, and *Just You and Me: A Magical Love Story.*

Upcoming novels by TN Jones: *That Young Hood Love, That Savage Love is Incredible, I Now Pronounce You, Mr. and Mrs. Thug,* & many more.

Thank you for reading the standalone, *Jonesin' For A Boss Chick: A Montgomery Love Story.* Please leave an honest review under the book title on Amazon's page.

For future book details, please visit any of the following links below:

Amazon Author page: https://www.amazon.com/tnjones666

Facebook: https://www.facebook.com/novelisttnjones/

Goodreads: https://www.goodreads.com/author/show/14918893.TN_Jones:

Google+: https://www.plus.google.com/u/1/communities/115057649956960897339

Instagram: https://www.instagram.com/tnjones666

Twitter: https://twitter.com/TNHarris6.

You are welcome to email her: tnjones666@gmail.com; as well as chat with her daily in her Facebook group, *Sipping and Chilling with Tyanna Presents* and *It'ks Just Me ....TN Jones*.